So Long, Honey
Aubrey Taylor

Copyright © 2024 by Aubrey Taylor

All rights reserved. No part of this publication may be reproduced, stored or transmitted in any form or by any means, electronic, mechanical, photocopying, recording, scanning, or otherwise without written permission from the publisher. It is illegal to copy this book, post it to a website, or distribute it by any other means without permission.

For permission requests, contact Aubrey Taylor, Aubreytaylorauthor@gmail.com

This novel is entirely a work of fiction. The names, characters and incidents portrayed in it are the work of the author's imagination. Any resemblance to actual persons, living or dead, events or localities is entirely coincidental.

Aubrey Taylor asserts the moral right to be identified as the author of this work.

Aubrey Taylor has no responsibility for the persistence or accuracy of URLs for external or third-party Internet Websites referred to in this publication and does not guarantee that any content on such Websites is, or will remain, accurate or appropriate.

Designations used by companies to distinguish their products are often claimed as trademarks. All brand names and product names used in this book and on its cover are trade names, service marks, trademarks and registered trademarks of their respective owners. The publishers and the book are not associated with any product or vendor mentioned in this book. None of the companies referenced within the book have endorsed the book.

Book Cover by Aurora McGaughey

Editing and Proof Reading by Becky Clapham

Illustrations by Aubrey Taylor

First Edition 2025

Contents

A Note from Aubrey	V
Epigraph	VI
Dedication	VII
Content Warnings	IX
Playlist	XI
1. CODY	1
2. CODY	7
3. FIELD	12
4. FIELD	18
5. CODY	25
6. FIELD	31
7. FIELD	38
8. FIELD	47
9. CODY	53
10. FIELD	59
11. CODY	66
12. FIELD	72
13. FIELD	78

14.	CODY	83
15.	FIELD	89
16.	CODY	95
17.	CODY	101
18.	CODY	107
19.	FIELD	112
20.	EPILOGUE	116
Acknowledgements		122

A Note from Aubrey

Hello Hornets,

The story you're about to read is of Ryan and Rae. While not main characters in the Hornets Nest Series, *they are two of the most important.*

This novella is meant to be enjoyed after Honey Pot.

Ryan and Lorraine shaped the Hornets together but separately. Running parallel courses with different views of what made a team, a winning team. Lorraine lead with love, kindness and compassion. She formed a family from a rag-tag group of young boys with the purpose of raising them to be gentlemen. She taught the Hornets how to survive, to cook and clean. To protect each other. Where as Ryan leads with quiet wisdom, stern guidance and sometimes what can be seen as cruelty.

But he was not always this way.

THIS IS HIS STORY.

AND ONE DAY THE GIRL
WITH THE BOOKS BECAME
THE WOMAN WRITING THEM

-KRISTEN COSTELLO

TO BUBBE
LOVE FOREVER YOUR
GRUMPY GROUCHER

CONTENT WARNINGS

PARENTAL ABUSE
EMOTIONAL & PHYSICAL
GRIEF/DEPRESSION REPRESENTATION
DISCUSSIONS OF TERMINAL ILLNESS
THE DEATH OF A LOVED ONE

TAKE BREAKS, GET SOME WATER,
SNUGGLE YOUR LOVED ONES AND PETS.

**BE KIND TO YOURSELF,
BEING A HUMAN BEING IS TOUGH.**

OFFICIAL PLAYLIST

FEELING THIS - **ALEX MELTON**
HONEY - **THE LONE BELLOW**
JESUS, ETC - **JOSIAH AND THE BONNEVILLES**
LITTLE BIT BETTER - **CALEB HEARN, ROSIE**
STOLEN LOVE - **JOSIAH AND THE BONNEVILLES**
COWBOYS CRY - **SASHA ALEX SLOAN**
BETWEEN THE COUNTRY - **IAN NOE**
NUMB - **TOMMEE PROFITT, SKYLAR GREY**
STARGAZING (MOONLIGHT VERSION) - **MYLES SMITH**
HEART LIKE A HOMETOWN - **KEITH URBAN**
MEET ME AT OUR SPOT - **CHRISTIAN FRENCH**
LIGHT MY LOVE - **GRETA VAN FLEET**
BEAUTIFUL ANYWAY - **JUDAH & THE LION**
EVERY LITTLE THING SHE DOES IS MAGIC - **SLEEPING AT LAST**
TO BUILD A HOME - **THE CINEMATIC ORCHESTRA**
SOMETHING I CANT AFFORD - **CIAN DUCROT**
I MISS YOU, IM SORRY - **GRACIE ABRAMS**
DEATH WISH LOVE - **BENSON BOONE**
NIGHT CHANGES - **ONE DIRECTION**
HERE (IN YOUR ARMS) - **HELLOGOODBYE**
GROWING SIDEWAYS - **NOAH KAHAN**
1435 - **SELFISH THINGS**
THE ROADS - **JONAH KAGEN**

AMEN - AMBER RUN

CODY

1996

"Ryan," Coach barked from the dugout. Veins burst from his neck as he screamed at me, and the reddish hue of his eyes deepened. "Swing hard, don't hesitate."

I shifted on my feet to quell the itch of adrenaline that rushed through my veins. There was quite literally nothing better than baseball. Sun poured from between the clouds into my eyes as the nervous pitcher relayed secrets to the catcher behind me. It didn't matter; it was mine once the ball left his mitt.

The crowd was buzzing like the thrum of an engine, louder than it had ever been. Loudest of all, my dad was above the noise, hollering instructions like I was playing T-Ball for the first time. It was frustrating how much he overstepped. I knew what I was doing; my skills weren't in question; it was my ability to focus.

A breeze tickled at my neck, causing strands of dirty blonde hair to brush my skin beneath my hat. Every tiny touch reminded me to draw attention to the ball, pitch, grass, and dirt. I needed to center myself in the moment. Inhaling slowly, I smelled the diamond and became a part of the atmosphere as the ball left his fingers and hurled toward me.

I stepped into the swing, my thigh flexing as my toes sunk into the sand and my biceps tightened. The crowd's applause grew tenfold as the ball connected with my bat and soared above the heads of the rival team. Gone far past the tiny fence of the high school field and smashed into the side of the bus, painted *Longhorns*.

The umpire called the home run, and lightning-like excitement exploded across my chest. I surged forward like a man possessed, hollering and cheering along with the crowd as I came across home plate completely uncontested. I turned, a smile flashing across my sweaty face, and winked at a screaming crowd of girls that huddled behind the backstop.

"You're a star, Ryan Cody."

One of them cooed at me, her pretty pink lips curled into a flirty smile and her big brown eyes drifting over me. She crossed her arm over her tiny waist and cradled her jaw in her long fingers as she leaned forward.

Her eyebrow arched, and she realized she had my attention. Curling her finger toward herself, she said, "Come here." She mouthed and nodded in encouragement.

I swerved toward them. I had no plan, but did I need one? *I was a star, after all*. My tongue flicked out over my lip, and I opened my mouth to say something stupid, no doubt when the collar of my jersey was tugged on so hard my feet kicked out from beneath me in the dirt.

"No." Coach's grip was so tight on the fabric that I could barely find my footing as he spun me around and pushed me over the catcher's box toward our dugout. "Game's not over, Cody. Celebrate later."

"Landry can hit without me watching," I whined. I attempted a sneaky escape as he released me, but the bat came up across the dugout exit, stopping me. "Oh, come on."

"Watch your teammate secure the win," he warned.

"I did that." My temper flared, and all the flirtatious feelings rushed from me as I squared my shoulders. "You and I both know it." The muscles in my jaw tightened as I stared him down.

Coach was exhausted. I could see it all over his old face. His once bright eyes were gray and void of any light. He was taking out his frustrations of being washed out on me. The long, harsh talks about making something for themselves scared the other guys. Preaching good grades and scholarships, but both of us knew I could make the Majors without school, without college.

"It pisses you off how good I am," I growled, knowing he wouldn't do anything in front of the entire school. "You're welcome for making this team great."

"Your ego will be the death of you, Cody."

Sure, maybe. I thought. *Probably.*

"At least I'll be happy when it happens. That's more than I can say for you."

He was dying a slow death coaching a bunch of spoiled kids who treated baseball like a hobby. The love of the game turned to dust before his eyes, coating his palms, and no matter how hard he tried, he couldn't scrub that feeling from his skin.

Coach opened his mouth to argue, but the umpire called Landry out as he rounded second base. Despite the lack of a run, we won the game by two.

Wrapping my fingers around the bat that prevented me from leaving the dugout, I pushed it away from me slowly, eyes never leaving Coach's.

"I'm a star, Coach." I smiled wide and threw my arms up.

Defeat flickered across his tired features, and confidence flushed mine, that cocky smile forming back on my face as I joined my teammates at the center for celebration. I could feel his eyes on my back, but it didn't matter. Ignorance was bliss. I needed a pretty girl to hold and a party to be thrown in my honor.

"Cody!" Landry screamed as his hat flew off his nasty red mullet and his hands thrust into the air. "Party at my house!" He declared, and the team went nuts. It wasn't unusual that the curly-haired, 200lb outfielder offered up his parent's massive house for a party. They weren't ever home, and Landry thrived on the sound of thumping bass through speakers that cost more than my house, as well as keg stands that would put the average man in the hospital for kidney failure.

The party continued through the evening, and the locker rooms were utterly trashed as we ran through them before taking the party back to Landry's mansion on the other end of town. Most of the guys on the team lived in the same gated community, big empty houses that rich people filled with kids they didn't want and never took care of.

I slipped from school to avoid my less-than-average farm-owning parents. There was always one sharp and stinging moment of guilt for disregarding their support for me, but it was easily passed with a kiss and pat on the back. Mom and Dad worked hard to put Riona and me where we were. Riona was on track to be the valedictorian and had barely escaped her freshman year in high school. She was going to make a difference in the world. One day, Robert Jr. would take over the farm; he and his wife Joanie lived in our attic. They had gotten married by the creek last summer, both barely twenty-one. But they were happy to be my parents' replacements. I could never understand why. To be stuck like that? It sounded like torture.

Baseball was it for me. I played better than any kid in the surrounding districts, and scouts were breathing down my neck six months after graduation. The more the pressure mounted on my shoulders, the more determined I became to be the best. I craved it and thrived off it. Unstoppable with the negative comments nipping at my heels and the sounds of cheering crowds roaring in my ears.

The party was spilling from the house by the time I got there, parking the truck down the street away from everyone else's car. I'd end up sleeping in Landry's guest room and didn't want my truck hit when some idiot decided to drive home drunk.

The house next to Landry's was always quiet, the lights always off, and I don't think I've ever seen a single person go in or out until tonight. She sat there, long dark hair spilling down her shoulders, her nose in a book as she scribbled something down and turned back to the telescope on the large, ornate porch. The moon bathed her in light as she searched the sky for something and returned to her notebook. She must have been an angel. No girl at school had ever... shone the way she was. Her skin was so perfect and soft, her lashes long enough to demand attention even at a distance.

I wanted to know her.

"What are you doing?" I stood on the sidewalk at the end of her driveway, holding my breath as she looked up at me.

I fought to stay standing as my heart skipped at beat from her glare, so tough and yet... it only made me want to get closer to her. *Who are you?*

"Go away." She shook her head and waved me off.

"You're the most beautiful girl I've ever seen," I exclaimed and stepped forward on the driveway, my ball bag still swinging over my shoulder as she collected her things into her arms.

"Are you deaf, I told you to leave!" She said.

My heart was beating so fast I swear it would have chased her through that closed door if I let it. "It would be a crime to leave you standing her all by yourself, you deserve to be admired a little longer." I laughed and scared myself with the sound of my voice. "Is it too soon for me to say I'm in love?" I asked her.

"I said, *go away!*" She repeated herself in a sturdy tone. Moon caught in those massive blue eyes as she stared just long enough for me to fall in love before she stomped into the house, slamming the door behind her.

Bee lining for Landry's, I pushed through the crowd, throwing my bag to the ground, and I found him in the living room on the couch. Two of the three girls from the game were tangled around him, hands in his hair and lips on his skin.

"Aye." I kicked his boot.

"Look who finally showed up!" Landry cheered, and the house followed suit! He pushed the girls off and thrust from the couch into my personal space, reeking of vodka and smoke. "Our shining star," he babbled and pinched my cheeks between his fingers.

"I should start charging for these celebrity appearances," I laughed and pushed his hands away from my face.

"We won't be able to afford you once you go to the show!" Landry hollered again, and the house erupted. "Let's get you a drink!"

"Hold on!" I pulled him back by the collar and stopped. "Who lives next door?" I asked him, my mind still on those eyes.

"Who cares!?" Landry laughed and threw his head back.

"*I care*," I said, ignoring the way everyone had started to watch us. I was used to having all the eyes on me. It didn't bother me in the least. Most of the time, I enjoyed the attention.

"Uh," Landry stumbled over his words, trying to remember. "The Fields," he said finally.

"Like *The Fields?*" I asked, grabbing him by the chin.

"Yeah, like Mayor Field, his hot wife, and their...weird, stuck-up mousy shut-in of a daughter, Lorraine."

Lorraine Field.

I chewed the inside of my lip and nodded.

"Why the hell do you wanna know about that mouse? She never leaves her house." Someone from our left piped up.

"Cause she's pretty and was on her porch," I snapped at no one in particular.

"Staring through that telescope?" Landry asked with an eyebrow raised. I could tell he was trying to piece it together but only confusing himself more as he tried. "She's a weirdo man, barely even goes to school."

"So you and her have a bunch in common, only she's attractive?" I teased and slapped his cheek playfully with my head.

"Ouch man," Landry scowled.

"Where's the keg?" I plastered a smile on my face, deflecting from the Lorraine conversation.

"There's my party animal!" Landry wrapped his arm around me and led me into the kitchen, each step a little further away from my unusual lingering thoughts.

CODY

"You're benched."

I pushed from my chair in the Coach's office. Principal McMaine stood off to the side behind the desk, staring at me with disdain on her crumpled old face.

"This is a joke, right?" I looked at them with utter dismay. I should have known something was off the second I stepped inside the office to find my father conversing with the two of them. "You're joking... okay." I shook my head.

"This isn't a joke, son," My father warned, his tone laced with authority. "Sit your ass down."

I listened. The only man able to demand anything from me was my father. His cold green eyes watched as I lowered into my chair. His face hardened from working under the Texas sun; he was all tan lines and calluses. His cowboy hat was shoved into his lap, and his messy, dirty blonde, graying hair was matted to his forehead with sweat.

"Your grades." Coach slid the folder across the table to me, "you're failing English, Ryan."

"No," I pushed my hat off my head and ran my fingers through my hair. "I've been getting passing grades on every paper I hand in."

"You've handed in three of the eleven assignments this semester, Mr. Cody." Principal McMaine nodded toward the folder with her eyebrows raised in disappointment.

I huffed, rubbing my hands over my jeans and leaning back in the rickety, tweed chair that itched at my biceps. "So what, I hand in those late assignments..."

"Missing," she corrected me.

"I hand in those *missing* assignments, and I'm clear."

"Not exactly," she explained. "You'll notice the absence of Mrs. Raymond?"

"Yes." I nodded.

Mrs. Raymond was a swamp creature.

Her long fingers scraped the chalkboard when she wrote her dull lectures across them for us to copy, and she smelled like bath water that a dog had been sitting in. We were all fortunate that Mrs. Raymond was absent. Coach would spend six weeks cleaning his carpets to get the smell out.

"Did she need to get home to check on her taxidermy collection?" I joked, but it didn't stick to the landing. "Ha, ha!"

"This isn't a joke, Mr. Cody." She stared at me.

My eyes flickered to Dad, who wouldn't even look out of sheer disappointment. It was written all over his face. His bearded jaw screwed shut because if he opened it out would spill a string of abuse that was only meant for the privacy of his old work truck.

"Mrs. Raymond has grown increasingly frustrated with your lack of care and respect in her class. She refused even to have this meeting with us. We're just trying to help you because if you don't pass this class, you won't play the rest of the season," she explained further.

The noose tightening around my throat at the thought of not playing ball anymore blurred my vision, and my breathing turned quick and shallow. Coach turned his eyes on me, pride burning behind them. This was punishment for making a fool of him yesterday, nothing more, but it was enough to shove back my panic.

"I'm impressed," I leaned back, masking the worry and forcing my tense shoulders to go slack as I crossed my arms over my chest. "You're willing to destroy the season for this?"

"This isn't my fault, Cody," Coach said without missing a beat.

"Mrs. Raymond has agreed to give you one more chance. You have two weeks to write a paper on something that matters to you. She's left a guideline, and Mr. Cody, this is your last chance. You'll take this seriously if you ever want to see the field again."

"Whatever." I shrugged my shoulders. The frustration rolled through me like a tidal wave. It was a mistake to bench me, and Coach would learn the hard way when the team started to lose without me. I wasn't going to beg on my knees for my spot. That's precisely what he wanted from me. "Can I go now?" I turned to Principal McMaine.

"You're excused."

I rose from my chair, scooping my bookbag in my fingers and over my shoulder.

"Mr. Cody," her voice hummed as I grabbed the door knob.

Turning back, I saw her, hand on her hip, folder in her hand, "You're forgetting something."

"Right," I said, taking the folder from her with a fake, cheesy smile and leaving the room as quickly as possible. The halls were empty as I turned out into them, making the hollow sound of my Dad's old cowboy boots stomping against the tile worse. He followed me toward the parking lot and out of the main doors.

"What the hell is wrong with you, boy?" He asked as we approached his truck.

"Nothing, it was a mistake." I looked around to ensure the parking lot was empty. "I'll get it straightened out."

His hand shot out and came down across the side of my head. The pain from the slap rang through my spine, shooting across my muscles in short, painful vibrations until it dulled and my eyes focused again.

"You have to take things seriously, Ryan. Do you think your mother and I work ourselves raw to support you and your sister so that you can throw it all away because you're too busy to hand in some stupid English assignment? You embarrassed me today." He grabbed the collar of my hoodie and slammed me against the truck.

"Dad," I said, wanting to push back but knowing I couldn't and probably shouldn't escalate the situation, at least not in public. "I'm trying."

"You've been acting like a child, sneaking out, pissing away your talent with drinking at that Landry house. You better smarten up, boy, and figure out how to act like a man, or I'll remind you how to."

His threats were never empty.

"I'll sort it out, Sir." I nodded tightly, "I have to go to class."

"Do not disappoint me," he warned, finally uncurling his strong hand from my hoodie. His finger came inches from my face, a warning. "I mean it, boy. Do not make me come back down here, or you'll never play ball again."

I heard him loud and clear.

Easier said than done.

He slammed the truck door and was gone before I could get my bearings. When I turned to look back up at the school, Lorraine Field was standing there. Her tiny, pretty face creased in concern as her fingers tightened around her books. The wind pushed through the long, dark strands of her brunette hair and danced around on her pale skin. She wore a long brown skirt and warm sweater that swallowed her frame whole.

Her bright blue eyes looked so sad in the daylight, and for a second, I forgot the ringing in my head.

She blinked, and a flash of heat rose to my neck.

"What are you staring at?" I barked at her, still on edge from my dad and now...embarrassed that someone had overheard that conversation.

She turned and started toward the school, forcing me to jog just to catch up to her.

"Fuck," I swore under my breath. "I'm sorry," I shook out the frustration, just trying to get her to stop for a second, but she only picked up her speed. "you're that girl from the porch!"

That didn't stop her, either. She reached for the door as I slid between her and it.

"I know you aren't mute," I teased, but she glared at me. I leaned into her space, watching her lean back. "Oh, come on, is this how you treat a boy hopelessly in love?"

"Excuse me," she said quietly, a rosy blush forming on her cheeks.

"That's it?" I exclaimed and leaned against the door as the bell buzzed over our heads. "How much of that conversation did you hear?" I asked her.

The look in her eyes told me everything I needed to know.

"He's not always like that," I brushed it off. "He's a pretty good dad. Your dad is the Mayor, right?"

"Sure," she blinked slowly, the disbelief evident as a tight scowl formed on her lips as she stared past me.

"You're very nervous," I noted, pressing against the door to give her space. "But very pretty."

"Can you move?" She hid the blush well, but I could see it creeping on her cheeks.

"Why haven't I seen you around before?" I asked her, shifting my bag on my shoulder and tilting my head into her eyeline with a bright, forced smile.

"Do you know where the library is?" She asked me.

I knew our school had one.

"Uh," I lifted my shoulders and tilted my head back, trying to find an answer.

"That's why," She said before I could, "now please move."

"You're not very friendly," I said.

"You're not very smart," she retorted, catching me off guard as she pulled on the door.

That time, I moved for her. A shred of insult hit home with her last remark, and the fight drained from my muscles. I watched her scurry down the hallway, expecting to feel relief when she turned the corner, but instead, I was flooded with the need to see her again.

FIELD

Mom was sitting at the table when I got home from school, her eyes dragging across whatever she was reading. I snuck through the kitchen and up the stairs to my room, dropping my book bag on the floor and curling into bed.

I had been uncomfortable since that morning, and despite doing my usual routine of class, volunteering in the office and library for an hour after lunch and again after school... I just couldn't shake the conversation I had overheard.

It wasn't my first time in that kind of position. Most people didn't notice when I was around, and it constantly put me in situations where I was left to overhear arguments and conversations I shouldn't, exactly like the one-sided argument between Ryan and his father. The pit in my stomach wouldn't let me forget the sound of Ryan's head hitting metal, no matter how hard I tried.

I wondered how many people knew about how his father treated him. It couldn't have been many if any at all. The way he had instantly tried to protect his father from criticism suggested he was emotionally carrying the blame for the abuse. A strained, guilty feeling overtook me when my thoughts wandered to what it was like having parents that hit you, and maybe it would be better than having ones that just ignored you.

At least they cared enough to be angry.

But that wasn't right. I was just mad at my situation and did not consider how horrible Ryan's experience was. Science suggests that stars form from a collection of gas and dust, which collapses due to gravity and starts to form stars. If Ryan were a star, the school, the teachers, the coaches, and his father would seemingly be at that gravity.

It was a lot of pressure to put on a seventeen-year-old.

The more I considered the situation, the more I was glad that my mother barely saw me. I kept my head down and worked hard, and one day, I'd be able to leave this town behind and make a life for myself that felt full. But not before my foolish teenage hormones overpowered every logical thought in my brain about a boy.

I rationalized each intrusive thought of Ryan Cody that brought a foolish smile to my lips or stirred around the butterflies in my stomach. He had seen me twice when I thought I was hidden from the world, and it was doing something to my brain and heart that I wasn't familiar with.

I chewed on my lip and slipped back out of bed, digging through my yearbooks until I found the one from the year before. I sank to the floor and flipped it open, finding his face quickly. His stupid dirty blonde hair was shorter than its current length, but his green eyes were as flirty and judgmental as ever. The air caught in my lungs, imagining the golden flecks that danced in the shades of green. High cheekbones, perfect cupid bow lips that curled into a devilish smirk that knotted in the pit of my stomach.

He had smiled at me like that today, turning my coherent thoughts into ribbons.

I liked being ignored because it saved me from ridicule. It was hard enough being the mayor's daughter without the attention of the High school star baseball player. I flipped through the book and found the team photo, finding him almost instantly in the front row. His shoulders were pinned back, and that same stupid smile on his face.

I slammed the book closed and tossed it back in the box.

He was just some dumb boy with a pretty smile. It meant nothing.

"Lorraine." A knock at the door made me jump.

I opened the door to my mother, her face stern and void of the normal olive tone she tans it to.

"There's a young man on our step," she said, and my brows furrowed.

"A boy?" I questioned.

"Yes, he claims he's here for tutoring," she explained, and I had only more questions.

"I'll be right down," I said.

"Lorraine," she used a tone that meant to *pay attention*. "You know the rules."

"No one in the house without an appointment," I groaned. This was a rule for my father, not for me, but somehow, I was always held to the same standards.

It's why I stopped trying to make friends. No one wanted to befriend the Mayor's daughter when they had to schedule a drop-in. When she disappeared from the hallway, I turned back to the mirror, unable to do anything about my mousy brown hair and exhausted-looking eyes. I chewed on my lip and took a deep breath.

It was unusual for anyone to show up on our doorstep, let alone a boy and one who was willing to lie to my mother's terrifyingly stern face. I took the back stairs and leaned around the banister blocking the front foray hallway. He couldn't see me, but Ryan Cody was in perfect view from my position. All six feet of him, with shaggy, wavy blonde hair. Those chunky bangs brushed against his temples as his green eyes surveyed his surroundings. His bookbag was over his shoulder, and his hands were in the pockets of his jeans as he waited.

"Send him away," I whispered to my mother as she rounded the corner adjacent to the kitchen.

"No," my mother shook her head. "That's not polite. Deal with your guest. You have homework to do."

Right. My mother wasn't a cold woman, but she was unbothered and uninterested in every facet of life that didn't contribute to our wealth or standing in the town. She had zero patience for disobedience and even less for strange men showing up on our doorstep. She'd feed me to the wolves if it meant protecting her sanity and reputation.

I straightened out, standing tall, and walked to the front door, grabbing the handle in passing to close it quickly and quietly. Ryan backed away as I approached like I might mean him harm and stopped about a foot from the stairs that led down the porch.

"What are you doing here?" I asked him through gritted teeth as I fought against the urge to tell him to go away. *Again.*

"Came to see the love of my life," He cooed, reminding me that I needed to scold him for doing so when my heart stopped racing at the sound of his voice.

"No one told you?" He looked around, huffing something under his breath before turning back to me. "Mrs. Raymond offered you up to tutor me in English. Apparently." He smiled, and the urge to shoo him away dulled more. "...You're the smartest girl in our class."

"And you're all bark," I countered. It was shaky and lacked confidence, but pushing him down a peg felt good.

"She does have a voice," he smiled brighter. "Alright, Mouse," he laughed. "It's true, though...look." I watched as he dug something out of an ivory school brand folder and handed it to me. It was a school-issued letter with the Longhorn logo and everything. Mrs. Raymond had even signed it.

"Told you." He winked at me.

"No." I handed the letter back to him. "I don't have the time."

"Now, don't take this the wrong way, but I know you have the time." He leaned back against the large white pillar. "Landry told me as much."

"Markus Landry is an idiot," I said, "just like every person that enters his house."

"Including me?" He cocked his head to the side.

"Especially you."

"Ouch, Mouse." He clutched his chest in his hand and pouted, "That was mean."

"Please stop calling me that," I asked him nicely. "I'm too busy to tutor you, but I'll talk to Mrs. Raymond in the morning and find someone else capable. I'm sure Carlos can help."

"Cooky Carlos?" Ryan shook his head. "That kid smells like cheese."

"And you're failing English, so I'm sure you'll be able to get past that. He's smart." I turned to go back into the house, but Ryan didn't move from the step.

"But not as smart as you," he added as I twisted the door knob.

"No."

"Then I want you," he said, and I turned to look at him.

"No," I repeated myself.

"Why not?" He whined, and the sound broke a wall down.

"Because you're cocky, rude, pushy, and frankly, I don't think you'd take it seriously, and it's not worth my time. Which, by the way, I don't have a lot of despite Mr. Landry's assumptions."

His green eyes took in my every word, never blinking or faltering as he watched me speak. His lips pressed together softly, and for a second, I thought maybe I had finally rendered him speechless.

But I had never been so wrong.

"So, would you like to do it here or at the library?" He asked.

I glared over my shoulder at him, ice in my veins that only fueled my annoyance.

"If we study in the library, everyone will see you getting tutored by the Mayor's daughter," I said.

He shrugged, "it's about time you got some attention."

"This isn't a joke," I warned him.

"That's the second time someone has said that to me today when I wasn't making a joke. I'm starting to think I'm not delivering these lines properly." He clicked his teeth together. "Listen, Mouse."

"Lorraine," I corrected him.

"Rae," he smiled.

"Lorraine," I groaned.

He nodded and stepped forward. He was so close I could smell the cologne he had sprayed on this morning, tangling with the sweat beneath his hoodie. "I'm taking this seriously. My career is on the line. If I don't figure out these papers and do it in the next two weeks. I'm benched for good. The game in Perrin is three weeks away. All the scouts will be there. I have to play in that game, Rae. If I don't, I'm stuck in this godforsaken town forever, and that can't happen."

I stared at him for a long moment, considering my options. I weighed my decision based on his words and his current position. He almost looked smaller as he spoke, pleading with me.

"I need your help," he said. "Please."

I'm stuck in this godforsaken town forever, and that can't happen.

I could hear the boy from this morning. The one that would say just about anything to his father to stop the public display of abuse. We both needed out for entirely different but very valid reasons.

"You meet me in the library every day at four," I said, and he smiled brighter than any star in the sky. "If you're even a second late, I'm done."

"Library, four o'clock." He repeated back to me with a few quick, nervous nods before he found his footing again. "Thank you for doing this."

"Don't thank me yet. You need to pass that class," I warned him.

"You need to have more faith in yourself, Rae."

I scowled, wanting to correct him again but slightly enjoying the elated feeling that purred in my chest when he called me that.

"Go away now," I said when he didn't leave my step.

"Alright." He put his hands up in mock surrender and stepped off the step. "I'll see you tomorrow, don't be late." His smirk was lopsided and hungry for attention.

"Get off my property, Mr. Cody," I narrowed my eyes at his joke and shook my head.

"Mr. Cody is my dad. You have to call me Ryan." He called from the driveway.

"In your dreams."

"You're right." His green eyes flickered with amusement as he nodded. "I'll see you there."

His causal nature clashed with my anxious demeanor. I stepped back into the house, closing the door behind me and resting my back against it as I caught my breath. A genuine smile formed as I thought about what he said, dreaming about me: no one had ever made me so flustered while simultaneously making me so frustrated.

I looked through the small window pane that framed the doorway and caught the last view of him before he turned the corner away from the gated community.

I'll see you there.

FIELD

It was two after four, and the clock in the library was louder than ever. Each second that passed by clicked loudly like someone was standing behind me, snapping their fingers in my ears. I stared down at the notes I had created for him. It had taken me hours after grabbing the missing assignments from his teacher and separating them in order of what would take him the longest to finish.

I hadn't gone to bed until three am.

Naïve idiot, I thought. His stupid smile and bright green eyes had burrowed deep into the back of my mind, giving me hope that he might not be as flaky and flirty as everyone said he could be.

That hope was shattered as the clock continued to mock me.

He was two hundred and forty seconds late.

I closed my book and stood from my chair, shoveling the books into my backpack as the doors to the library slammed open. Ryan skittered in like a wet cat, out of breath and frantic. His eyes widened as he watched me pack up my book, jogging over to the table with his hand out to stop me.

"You're late," I said.

"I love you too, beautiful." He smiled out of breath, pulling his hand out from behind his back with a bundle of flowers. "I got these for you."

"Whose garden did you steal them from?" I asked, trying to ignore the fact that he had called me beautiful. *Again.*

"I paid a garden club nerd five dollars to let me raid the greenhouse, so I'm late." He set them down when I didn't take them and dropped his bag on the floor, moving around the desk to my side.

"That's not a good enough excuse." I shook my head and continued to pack my bag when he dropped to his knees beside me and closed the opening with his hands. "Get up," I whispered at him angrily as a few of the other students started to turn and look at the commotion.

"Not until you forgive me for being late," he pouted, those big green eyes on fire under the harsh fluorescent lights of the library. "Come on, Mouse. I'm sorry. I just wanted to do something nice for you, but it backfired." He flipped his cap off and pressed it to his chest, still staring up at him with those long lashes.

"I told you not to call me that." I shook my head, wanting to deny him, to send him away, and to let him fail, but it was hard to say no to Ryan Cody, especially when he was staring at me like that, causing a scene in the library.

"Listen, Rae, I need you. Do you understand that? This is life or death for me. You hold my entire future in your pretty little hands." He said.

I chewed my lip, worried that the entire situation was slipping from my fingers, but I nodded, "Fine, just get off the damn floor, stupid." I hissed.

Ryan chuckled and pushed off his knees as he ran his hand through his messy sandy blonde hair. Those damned strands framed his flirty eyes, and the heat rose to the back of my neck.

I shook off the feeling of warmth and took my book back out, dropping it on the table next to the flowers he had brought me. The flower that secretly made me feel special and that I would attempt to keep alive for as long as possible as soon as I left today.

"I separated all your assignments to make them more manageable. We'll get as many as we can do in the next two weeks, and hopefully, if we get enough of them done, you'll be able to play again," I explained to him.

"Hope is fickle," Ryan said, "I need your guarantee," he said, looking up from the binder.

"Whether or not you finish these papers isn't up to me. You have to put in the work, Ryan. I can't do that for you," I said with a tiny shrug.

"Say my name again," he hummed, tilting his chin.

"No." I shook my head, ignoring how my body reacted to his attention. "Pay attention. Start with this one," I pointed to the easiest of them all.

"I hate that one," he groaned and slid into his chair, moving it over so he was shoulder-to-shoulder with me. He caved when I stared at him with a deep scowl. "Alright, alright, Mouse, you're gonna burn a hole in me."

I huffed at his nickname and watched as he pulled out his pencil and paper, slowly starting to read the assignment notes. "I don't understand what's so educational about writing a paper on a childhood memory."

"It's about reflection on your life. It's about your ability to recount, not the memory." I shrugged, separating the emotion from it.

"So she wants me to write a memory but doesn't care about it just so that she can judge my ability to tell a story?" Ryan laughed, eyes flashing up to meet mine as I nodded. "That's absurd."

"It's just a memory," I said. "It should be easy; pick a favorite of yours."

Ryan's hand paused the nervous tapping he had started. Seeing how his father treated him, I realized there might not be as many as I had assumed, and for once, we were standing on level ground. I inhaled slowly, trying to find a way out of the corner I had backed him into accidentally. Our stories weren't the same. I had never been...hit. I had never had a reason to think about it before, but being ignored was better than being abused.

"What's your favorite?" He asked me.

"This isn't about me," I said quietly. *I didn't have any.*

"Mrs. Raymond isn't going to know the difference," Ryan said.

"You aren't starting this paper by plagiarizing someone else's life," I sighed.

"Just give me an idea, Mouse. Maybe then I can make something up." He shrugged. He was doing anything he could to avoid digging deep into his childhood, and it made my heart ache for him.

"What about a baseball memory?" I asked him, and he sank his teeth into his bottom lip, and his gaze became distant.

"Let's do a different one. I'm sure I'll think of something eventually." He flipped the pages in the binder to the next one. The following six assignments he had missed were all topics involving him as a person, his memories, his family, and simple issues for normal kids, but they all seemed to make his skin crawl. Suddenly, I understood that there was a deeper issue as to why he was failing English.

"Didn't you win that award last year?" I flipped the binder back to the first assignment and tapped the title. "For being really good at baseball?"

"Most Valuable Player," he chuckled, but it was hollow and unexpected. "They would give those out to anyone. It's just a pat on the back."

"But they gave it to you," I said.

"Only because I scored a home run in the last inning with loaded bases, winning us the game," he made it sound so easy, so carefree, and it wasn't the Ryan that he projected to everyone else.

"Oh," I swallowed, trying to devise a plan on the fly. "So you're saying you're average?"

This time, Ryan laughed genuinely and shook his head gently before looking up at me. "I'm far from average, Mouse. I'm god damn incredible."

"So you should have a story to tell," I poked back at his inflated ego, how easily it had been to find it beneath his concrete walls. "You talk more than any boy I've ever met."

"You talk to a lot of boys, Rae?" He asked, sliding his face into his palm as he watched me. I hated how much I loved the attention.

"I'm not a shut-in, Ryan," I said and watched him swallow tightly at the sound of his name on my lips. Even more so, I hated how much I enjoyed making him squirm.

"That I don't believe. I've never seen you at a single party," he said, completely distracted from his work.

"You're supposed to be writing a memory," I said, tapping the paper.

"Tell me the last fun thing you did, and I'll write," He challenged me.

I stared him down, trying to figure out a reasonable answer he would deem appropriately fun enough to start his paper. Why I was even buckling to his bargaining was beyond me.

"Last semester, the yearbook club threw a wrap party," I said.

"What did you do?" Ryan asked.

"Uh—we went bowling." I shrugged.

"You went bowling?" He laughed so hard he nearly fell from his chair. "Rae, that's not fun. That's organized torture."

"It was fun…" I said with a small grumble. "I scored a perfect game."

He set down his pencil and leaned forward on the desk with a bark of laughter. "How do you even score a perfect game in bowling? You gotta explain this to me!"

"I'm sorry that it wasn't getting drunk in Landry's backyard and throwing up in a bush!" I covered my face with my hands and sighed. "That was the last fun thing I did. Now, do your work."

"Not until you tell me how you scored a perfect score," he said with that perfectly lopsided grin. "And for the record, I haven't puked in a bush since junior year!"

"So talented," I mocked him.

"Says the bowling Queen of the Wild West," Ryan scoffed.

"You score all strikes. Across the board, there's no science to it." I shrugged and threw his pencil at him. "Work."

"There's no way you bowl perfect strikes. That's impossible," he laughed.

"It's very possible, and I can do it. It's just math."

"You are so very serious right now," Ryan's tongue darted out over his bottom lip, and he nodded, seemingly impressed. "You'll have to show me one day, Mouse."

"No. Do your work. I have to be home for dinner in half an hour." I said tightly.

"Can I walk you home?" He asked me, ignoring my order to finish his work.

"No," I said.

"Why do you hate me so much?" He whined and blew out a huff of air.

"Because you're exactly the kind of boy I've been avoiding the entirety of high school, and now I'm stuck tutoring you in a class you don't respect so you can win your big match and get laid."

"Whoa now," he put his hands up, "I can get laid without winning a ball game."

I practically growled at his response. "Could you take this seriously for two minutes?"

"I'm over it," he leaned back in his chair and studied me. I was growing increasingly frustrated with his flippant attitude toward the work. "Listening to you talk about your bowling escapades is far more interesting."

"If you aren't working on your assignments, then there's no point to this tutoring," I looked him over, grabbing my binder, but he reached out and stopped me. "I'm not going to sit here and let you make fun of me, Mr. Cody."

"Oh, stop it," Ryan shook his head, "don't go back to the Mr. Cody crap."

"You're treating this like a joke, and I have things to do." I scoffed, pushing back from the table.

"I'll do the assignment tonight. I don't want to sit here scribbling down some fake memory while you stare at me like I'm an idiot. I would rather use the time to *talk to you*." He said.

"You *are* an idiot," I stood up. "This is about you passing that class so you can play in your big, important, life-changing game, Mr. Cody. It's not about me."

"I hate when you call me that," he pouted but stood up.

"I hate it when you don't do your assignments." I shook my head and slung my bag over my shoulder, preparing to walk home. As I left the library, I could feel him on my tail, "What are you doing?" I spun around to look at him.

"Walking you home." He said, his hat back over his hair and his chin tucked down into his sweater as he followed behind me at a distance.

"I told you no," I said.

"For someone so smart, you sure don't figure stuff out very quickly. I'm a *bad* listener."

I sighed, staring at him for a moment longer.

"You better hurry, Mouse. You'll be late for dinner." He said, cocking his head to the side with a serious look on his face.

He had stayed true to his words and walked me all the way home, almost right up the driveway, before ensuring I was inside. Dinner was boring. Mom grilled me on my whereabouts after school, and I had to fork over the letter from Mrs. Raymond about the tutoring before she left me alone.

Dad didn't bother to show up.

I spent most of the night in my room focusing on homework that had briefly been neglected until a knock on the door pulled my attention from the book.

"That young man is back on our porch, Lorraine. I thought you understood the rules," Mom said in a cold, authoritative tone. My heart was pounding in my chest, thinking she might do something about it herself, but part of me knew she would never make a scene—not the mayor's wife. Never. I nodded and slipped off the bed.

"I'm not sure why he's there, but I'll send him away," I said, moving past her toward the stairs. I stopped in the hallway to ensure my sweater covered my chest before opening the door and stepping into the chilly air.

Ryan jumped from his spot on the bench and closed his book over, extending his hand to me. "Here," he held a small stack of papers covered in his messy handwriting. "I finished."

"How long have you been out here?" I asked him.

"Since you left me," he said. I looked down at the watch on my wrist, six hours. He had been out there for *six hours*.

I scowled, backing away from him and wandering inside without a word. I walked to the kitchen, collected the glass pan with the leftover lasagna inside and a fork, grabbed a pop can, and carried it back outside. He was slumped on the bench, pouting, no doubt thinking I was still mad at him.

"Eat," I said, almost dropping the pan in his lap.

"I'm not a charity case, Rae. I just wanted to finish this," he waved the paper at me.

"You eat, I'll read it," I said, sitting quietly on the bench beside him.

CODY

A few days later, I knocked on the door sometime after dinner, knowing I might get her in more trouble than she was already in for spending time with me. When the door swung open, and she shooed me back off the porch down onto the steps, I knew I had fucked up.

"What are you doing?" She questioned in the most adorable, whispered, angry voice.

"I just wanted to know if I loved you more on Saturdays," I shrugged, letting it slip out before I could stop myself. I couldn't help it. I craved the blossom pink color, saying it always turned her freckle-stained face. I could tell she had been eating cherries; her lips were darker than usual, and her fingertips were a funny-tinged color.

"Ryan!" She growled.

"I came to take you for a walk. I got out of my chores and wanted more homework done. The second paper is calling our name." I insisted.

She watched me momentarily, gauging my words with the weight of what she knew about me. A walk felt too innocent, and my wanting to do homework on a Saturday felt even less. On a surface level, the request was odd, but if she knew how fast my heart thudded in my chest every time I saw her, she wouldn't question my motives. I wanted to be around her constantly, even if it meant doing homework.

"Are you sure?" She asked him.

"Positive," I said.

She chewed on her cherry-stained bottom lip for a moment longer, tucking a strand of her dark hair back off her face. I opened my mouth to argue the point and convince her further, but she cut me off with a simple "Okay." Before she shuffled back inside, she left me on the step.

I fiddled with the sleeves of my shirt, tugging at the loose threads while my heart tried to claw its way out of my chest. I fixed my unruly hair in the window, taking note of the pristine white-washed living room on the other side of the blurred reflection.

My dirty baseball T-shirt and mud-stained jeans stood out like a sore thumb. I was painfully aware that a guy like me could never be good enough for a girl like Lorraine Field, but if she would even allow me in her orbit just for a little while, I would take all the time I could get.

"Are you ready?" She asked, breaking me from my trance. I hadn't heard her come back outside, but her hair was pulled into a ponytail, and she had slipped into a pair of jeans and an oversized sweater that hid her from me.

"Let me," I surged forward as she went to throw her backpack on. Our hands brushed together as I reached for the strap, and she flinched back from me. I flexed my hand tightly, slowly reducing my movements so I didn't spook her, and slipped the strap from her shoulder.

"Can I?" I asked, holding up my loose binder. She nodded, allowing me to stuff it in her little bag before I hoisted it over my shoulders and stood up straight. "Come on, I want to show you something."

Lorraine hesitated initially but eventually followed me as we walked down the street away from her house and out of the gated community she was sequestered in. She looked nervous. The way she crossed and uncrossed her arms gave her away worse than the worried look on her face.

"I promise you'll like it," I told her, trying to close the gap and ease the trees' silence filling the air. We crossed down through town, where most of the shops were closing up for the evening. The streets emptied, and the sky became heavy with oranges and purples.

"Absolutely not," she stopped dead when she saw the entry to the path. "I might not get out much, but I know where that goes." Lorraine shook her head.

I had known that getting her to go down the path that led to the infamous make-out spot would be difficult, so I had come prepared with reasoning.

"We aren't going to the make-out spot," I told her, and she narrowed those pretty blue eyes at me like they could inflict damage. "There's a separate path halfway down that takes you up the hill to the other side. It's covered, and no one knows, but I want to show you something. So don't be such a coward."

"A coward?" She gawked at me.

"I am not a coward, Mr. Cody. I'm sorry if traipsing around in the dark with a boy whose reputation is anything but gentlemanly is concerning." She shook her head and crossed her arms again.

"Rae, I'm not trying to steal your innocence," I laughed and extended my hand to her, wiggling my fingers at her. "I promise you'll enjoy it. Just take a chance."

Lorraine pressed her lips together in a thin line and looked around at the woods that engulfed us before she blew a small breath. "I have a pocket knife in my backpack, and I swear I'll use it on you, " she said with conviction.

"I believe it," I laughed as she took my hand, and I pulled her down onto the path. As I said, the path broke off into a smaller trail blocked by a slight covering of tree branches. I lifted them gently and allowed her to pass beneath my arm, smelling the fruity shampoo that wafted up from her air as she did. I stayed close behind her, our bodies bumping into each other occasionally as she got nervous or unsure about the path ahead. "And for the record, I'm a perfect gentleman and never kiss a girl unless she asks me to."

Her body stiffened slightly at my joke but continued moving down the trail.

"Just a little further," I pointed over her shoulder, leaning down to whisper in her ear; I felt her body tense at the closeness.

Lorraine nodded and continued on steady, tiny steps toward the small opening in the trees ahead of us. As we approached, I heard her small gasp as she realized that the fear and nervousness was all worth it.

The overlook was empty, surrounded by thick trees, and completely hidden from the town. We stood on a small cliff side that looked down over the twinkling lights of small-town Texas, and Lorraine's eyes were alight with wonder.

"I didn't think—" She stopped, inhaled gently as she stepped forward.

"Careful, that's a far drop." I reached out for her arm and tugged her back a bit, setting down her bag and coming to stand next to her. "That's not even the best part," I laughed. The sun was swallowed by the horizon, and above us, the sky had started to go dark, truly dark. Without the bothersome buzz of street lamps and town lights, the sky was left to illuminate the forest on its own.

"The stars," she gasped, her head tilting up so far that I thought she might fall over if she didn't stop straining. My hand gently pressed against her lower back. She was too busy enjoying the stars to notice my hot gaze on the side of her face, taking in every moment of pure, unbridled wonder.

"They're so bright," she whispered to the sky.

"You're always staring up at the sky through that telescope," I said, like it mattered.

Lorraine was lost in the stars.

She stared there, frozen in place, as the rest of the sun disappeared, leaving the valley in darkness, and I just let her. I often came up here just to escape from my Dad screaming across the ranch, angry at the cows for being cows and the grass growing sideways. Sometimes I felt like that grass. It was exhausting, and most days, I needed to clear my head before ball games to even concentrate.

"You can see Eta Carinae from here," she whispered, her eyes trailing to the sky. "It's hard to see; for a long time, it wasn't visible at all, but recently, it's started to shine brighter in the sky, and soon you'll be able to see it so clearly."

"Where?" I asked her over her shoulder, and she lifted her hand, pushing on my chin until I was looking at what she could see. "That star?" I asked.

"It's not just one star. It's two; they've been unstable for years, and if all the information we have on her is correct, the two stars will eventually supernova together and die."

"That's sad," I whispered, and she turned to look up at me, her face so close to mine.

"It's not if they collide and supernova. They'll be together forever. It's romantic."

I couldn't think straight with her lips so close to mine, and I had never been in a position where the thought of kissing a girl made me nervous. I inhaled slowly, "you'll have to explain to me how two stars dying is romantic, Mouse."

She pressed her lips into a thin line, "don't mock me."

"I'm not," I said so quietly that only she and the stars heard me. "Tell me."

"It's romantic because even the most unstable star found someone to share the sky with."

We watched each other for the longest minute of my life, simple and soft, before her brows pulled in tightly, and she went back to being irritated by my presence.

"How are you supposed to do a paper in the dark?" She finally asked, and it pulled a genuine loud laugh from my chest. "I'm not doing homework on a Saturday."

"Ryan," she scolded.

"I had to get you away from that museum you call a mansion and into the fresh air." I shrugged. "Lying was the only way you were going to trust me."

"That's contradicting." Lorraine shook her head and stepped back from me.

"But God, was it worth it," I said, staring at her framed in the soft purples of the darkening sky and the twinkling lights of the shining stars. I let out a tiny huff of air at her beauty, brighter than any of the stars in competition. I had walked down that street looking for a party and a drunken night but stumbled straight into love. Stupid as it sounded, I knew it was love because I had never felt that way about anything in my entire seventeen years of life. Not even about baseball. Lorraine Field was the only thing that mattered.

"I don't understand you, Ryan Cody." She scowled at me. "One moment you're insufferable, loud, and annoying, and the next..."

"The next what?"

"You're quiet and charming, it's..."

"Contradicting?" I offered with a small smile.

"Extremely," she said with a scrunch of her nose, and my hands flexed at my side, resisting the urge to smooth out the lines of her worried face. "Our relationship is a forced transaction, Ryan. I have to tutor you, and you have to pass English. I don't know why you're trying so hard to make something of that. I don't need your attention even if you're disguising it for friendship, and I don't know what you're trying to get at, but I'm not like those girls that fawn over you. I never will be."

She watched me momentarily, waiting for me to argue with her, maybe? Or tell her everything she wanted to hear, maybe even spin some version of the truth she was digging for? But there weren't any ulterior motives. There wasn't a secret plan to get in her pants or embarrass her. There was just her and the incessant need to be around her.

"You don't *need* the attention, but you deserve it, Rae," I said with a slight nod.

"I don't understand how you came to that conclusion," she said.

"You could have told me to go away that day on your porch," I said.

"I did," she scoffed. "*Twice*."

"You could have meant it, but you didn't. And you didn't again when I came to you for help or when you fed me dinner..." I licked my bottom lip and stepped closer to her. "It's okay to enjoy the company of others for something other than a transaction; you aren't wasting time or potential when you stop to enjoy the stars."

I could see the thoughts swirling behind her glassy blue eyes. Her life had been perfectly curated around her but never for her. She had a perfect house with a perfect little family, but deeper down, somewhere inside her, a girl needed fun and freedom.

Just like the boy in me needed kindness and structure, we fit together like a sharded piece of glass—or, instead, two unstable stars colliding.

"You are a very confusing boy, Ryan."

"You'll get used to it, Rae."

FIELD

The air outside was growing warmer with every passing day, and the dry temperatures made my head dizzy. I should have sat inside at the table with my book, but the sky was a pretty orange color and clear as ever. Once the sun went down, it would be a perfect night for stargazing.

I took a sip of water and set it back on the table beside the porch bench, trying to let the foggy feeling pass without having to call my Mom for help inside. I chewed on my lip, saying a silent prayer that it was temporary nausea from the heat.

With my head in my book, I heard him approach up the driveway and climb the stairs without ever acknowledging his presence.

"Two more papers done." He set the stack down on the bench next to me. "Let me take you to the fair?"

"No," I said.

"You love that damn word, say yes," he chuckled.

"No." I didn't look up from the book I was reading, even as he hovered. "If you don't leave soon, my mother will see you, and you'll wish you had listened when I told you to go away the first time."

"Let me take you to the fair, Rae," he said again and finally, I looked up at him. "*Please.*"

Gold danced across those big green eyes, and all I wanted to do was say yes to him. But the school fair? That was one place I wasn't comfortable. It wasn't for kids like me. It was loud, bright, and full of people who just saw right through me.

Ryan dropped down into a squat, both of his hands gripping to the bench, effectively caging me in on either side with his arms. "I know exactly what you're doing inside that pretty little head of yours," he said, chin tilted toward me. "You're thinking, I don't belong at a place like a school fair, that's for the cool kids, I'm not popular enough or pretty enough."

I opened my mouth, and he narrowed his eyes.

"But riddle me this," he said, "why would I want to go to the fair with anyone but the beautiful girl who stole my heart? It seems futile and boring."

There he went again, using that stupid word like it meant anything to him other than vapid flattery. But his jaw clenched tightly, and his fingers dug into the bench as he waited for my answer.

"I want to take you on the Ferris wheel, Lorraine Field and you can't stop me." He added when the silence stretched on for too long.

"It's—" I said and stopped, "my parents will be there."

Something similar to insecurity flickered across his expression, an emotion I had never seen before from him. He is usually so confident and unshakable. It was like the day in the parking lot, standing before his dad, just trying to look smaller so the moment of anger would pass.

"Fine," I said, refusing to use the word yes just to spite him. "But no Ferris wheel, I'm terrified of heights."

"There's no way the girl who dances with the stars is afraid of heights," he said so effortlessly that my mouth fell open, and a sly smirk formed on his face.

"There's a difference between studying the stars through a telescope and being spun around in the air at sixty feet, Ryan," I said to him.

"I'll hold your hand. You'll be okay." He said softly and for a split second I believed him. But then I realized that taking his hand wasn't just for me. It was to steady his own steps as well. I slotted my hand into his and let him pull me from the bench. "I like it when your hair is messy," he looked at me, now hovering and looking down at me with that same stupid smile that makes my stomach roll with unbridled nerves. "And when you get nervous," he said quietly, "your cheeks get warm, and your shoulders pin back like you're trying to stop it from happening."

There was nothing I could say in response without a jumble of words leaving my mouth that didn't make any sense. Ryan Cody had me in knots, and I absolutely hated it.

"Are you taking me to the fair or not?" I grumbled, trying to pass off the intense feelings that rumbled through me to my toes.

"Go put a sweater on. It's supposed to get cold tonight," he said in a hushed breath.

I hated his stupid tan and freckled skin, his sharp jaw, and bright green eyes, which reminded me of Christmas trees. I pushed back from his gravity, ignoring the undeniable pull of him, and marched inside, closing the door behind me. When I returned, he was standing in the same place I had left him, in his navy blue hoodie, a backward hat that hid the messy strands of dirty blonde hair, and ugly old tattered cowboy boots tucked into his shabby blue jeans. It was such a simple outfit, and for some reason, he looked so handsome. I couldn't help but smile at him before locking the door behind me.

"You ready, Starlight?" He asked.

The nickname made my breath hitch, "what happened to 'mouse'?"

"It didn't suit you, you're not a mouse, you're a star. I didn't know you. *Now I do*. Chalk it up to human error." He shrugged. *Starlight*, I chewed on my bottom lip and begged the nervous sparks to fizzle out.

"So, are you ready?" He asked again.

I wasn't, I don't think I ever would be, but saying no would only have him bothering me even more for answers I didn't have and couldn't come up with when I was so damn distracted.

"Yeah," I said instead, "I'm not riding the Ferris wheel."

"We'll see," he said and stepped down the step backward, watching every step I took.

I wanted to tell him how uncomfortable he made me, but I knew it would only make him happy. He wanted me riled up, confused, and blushing, and I hated every second of it. We walked along the pristine pavement toward the large security office and gate of my community. I waved to Roger, who sat reading a comic book with his upper lip covered in pasta sauce. He pressed the button to let us out with that same familiar smile he always had on.

Ryan led me a little ways down before side-stepping with his arms out. " You chariot, my Starlight, " he hummed.

And for the first time, I didn't want to scold him for the nickname. I enjoyed how it rolled off his tongue and the toothy grin that always seemed to follow it up. My heart swelled at seeing his pickup truck, blue and white paint peeling around the burnt orange rusty tire wells and the crooked rear view mirror in the windshield.

"That's a death trap," I offered him a genuine smile.

"Don't talk about *Baby* like that," he huffed, "you'll hurt her feelings."

"You named that rust bucket," I giggled, and Ryan's head snapped toward me. At first I thought he was mad or offended, but his eyes twinkled, and his brows flinched slightly as his head cocked to the side. "What?" I asked.

"I don't think I've ever heard you laugh," he said in a hushed tone.

"I laugh all the time," I argued as he opened the passenger door for me.

"No, you don't," he paused before closing the door behind me, his fingers wrapped around the frame as he stared at me with a serious look on his handsome face and his his tone dropped an octave. "I would remember that sound."

Ryan shut the door before I had time to respond, but I could feel my cheeks turning red again, and I was starting to think about my decision to go to the fair with him. If anyone saw us there, it would be hard to find an excuse for it. Worse, if my parents saw us, I would be in so much trouble I would never hear the end of it.

I slumped into the bucket seat as Ryan started the engine and drove us down the windy hill toward the school. The committee had used the football field to set up despite the football coaches' protests about it ruining the field.

Lights flickered and twinkled in the night air, lighting the center of town up like a firework under the pitch sky. I had never been to the fair, never seen its appeal. The smell of fried foods and sweet, sticky cotton candy in the air combined with the shrill laughter of an overwhelming crowd.

"Take me home," I panicked a little as he parked.

"Okay," he said without hesitation, which caused me to turn to him suspiciously. "If you don't want to be here, Rae, I'm not going to force you," Ryan said.

"I—" I started and stopped, rubbing my hands over my jeans only for him to catch one of them with his own. I tensed at his sudden touch and looked down as his fingers wrapped around mine.

"I can take you home, and you can show me more stars," he shrugged like it wasn't a bother like he hadn't just dragged me all the way down in excitement. And now, without even a fuss, he was willing to take me all the way home.

"Why would you do that?" My brows furrowed.

"Because you asked," he said so simply that it felt as though the world had come crashing down around the truck, and there were just the two of us left.

"That's silly," I said.

"No, it's not. It's polite and...kind, and I'd do just about anything to make sure you're happy," he argued, untangling our hands and flicking his finger beneath my chin. Tingling livewires surged under my skin from his touch, and I trained my gaze on his. "If you want to go home, I'll take you home. But," he licked his bottom lip and leaned over the center of the bench into my space. "I think you're just scared, and if that's the case, then please give me a chance to show you how much fun we can have?"

My eyes flickered from him to the blurry lights in the background just beyond. Sickening nerves bubbled up to the surface and threatened to ruin his sweater, but I nodded.

"Yeah?" he said softly, and I nodded again. "That's my brave little star," he praised, and for whatever reason, a tiny whimper left me. Whether it was fear or shock, it made him laugh. "Come on, first, you have to eat."

"Isn't that a horrible idea before rides?" I asked, finding my voice as he unbuckled my seatbelt and reached over me to pop the door open.

"So innocent," he mumbled, shooing me out, sliding across the bench and following behind. "Driver-side door doesn't open from the inside," he laughed and jumped down onto the pavement beside me.

He walked a few steps before realizing I wasn't following and stuck his hand out to me, "stay close," he said, wiggling his fingers at me. Something I noticed he did often, and as childish as it felt at first, it always made me feel comfortable enough to take his hand.

Just as expected, the football field was packed. The rides and booths created narrow paths through the grass that hundreds of bodies funneled through.

"I didn't even know the town had this many people," I yelled over the sound of a horn blasting from one of the nearby games.

"Aren't you the school treasurer?" He looked over his shoulder at me as we weaved through a crowd of people.

"Yeah, but..." I shrugged. The fact that he knew that made the butterflies in my stomach go wild.

"Pretty sure this fair brings in more revenue than all the other school events," Ryan tugged me out of the way of a girl juggling a bottle of pop and a bear twice her size. "You really have never come?"

"It's not my thing," I said. It's bad enough to feel invisible in the high school hallways, but there was a new level of transparency. It was like I didn't exist. But with my fingers intertwined with Ryan's, and his eyes locked in on mine. I wasn't invisible. Not tonight.

"Popcorn, corn dog, or snow cone?" He asked.

I looked around at my options and sighed. I was usually allowed popcorn, and snow cones were sugary. "Corn dog," I said, not realizing it was out loud, but a determined smile spread across his face.

"One corn dog coming up," he shifted his grip and darted through the crowds with me on his tail until we came to a line of carts that wafted with an overwhelming fried dough smell. He ordered one, paid the kid working the booth, and held it out for me.

"What, no mustard?" I looked down at it, and Ryan barked a boisterous laugh that made people stare as the heat rose up my neck. He turned back to the kid and asked for assistance before returning with the corn dog in better shape. "Thank you," I said quietly, taking a bite of the warm dough.

Ryan stared at me as I sunk my teeth into it, his fingers tapping the napkin wrapped around the tail end of it as I chewed. "So?" He asked.

"It's delicious," I licked my lips as he took a bite for himself and groaned with happiness.

"I would have preferred a snow cone," he laughed and offered me more.

My eyes drifted to the space just behind him, where a group of girls watched my every move with horrible snarls on their pretty faces. My fingers twitched at my sides with nerves as Ryan blissfully enjoyed the corn dog, utterly unaware that we were being observed.

"Ignore them," he said with a mouth full of hotdog, "they all share one brain."

Maybe not so unaware.

"It's a very cruel brain they share to gossip," I added, my eyes still nervously trained on them.

"They're just jealous, Starlight," he mumbled. He gave me the last bite of the corn dog and chucked the garbage. I focused on the girls when he came up behind me and rested his hand on my hip.

My entire body tensed under this grasp as his chin found home on my shoulder, "you picked the snack. I picked the ride."

"Ryan, I don't like heights," I reminded him.

"Have I let you down so far?" He asked, his breath fanning on my cheek as I shook my head no.

"Good, Ferris wheel it is."

FIELD

I wanted to dig my heels into the soft grass as Ryan shimmied us through the crowd toward the lineup for the massive turning wheel. My hands were trembling by the time we came to a stop behind a few others in the line.

"I don't think I can," I exhaled a shaky breath and stared up at the ride.

"I know you can." Ryan shrugged like it was as simple as that, as if I wasn't turned inside out with fear over sitting on the rickety, swaying buckets. "Rae," he said, snapping me from my terrified trance. "Take my hand," he said, and I listened without protest as he led us up onto the unbalanced steel structure and into a two-person bucket that rocked as we said down.

I shut my eyes tightly and dug my fingers into the top of his hand as the bar came down across us, and the ride jolted to life. Ryan sat quietly beside me, not saying a word as the breeze rustled our hair and bit our cheeks.

"Open your eyes," he said to me, but I just shook my head. I was too scared to open my eyes and see how high we had climbed. "I'm right here. Nothing bad will happen."

"You can't actually promise that because there are about ten thousand things that could go wrong up here," I said, screwing them shut as tightly as possible.

"Like what?" Ryan laughed and nudged me with his shoulder, causing the bucket to shudder and me to yelp. "I'm sorry," he huffed with a chuckle and sat still.

"Like the fact that there are no proper restraints on this ride!" I said with a tiny huff as a gust of wind rattled us around. "Extended in the air like this…" My hands trembled as it kicked up again, and the ride came to a rickety halt. "The wind is stronger, and how am I supposed to trust a giant ride put together by people who never graduated high school!"

"Please, Starlight, don't stop. This is the loudest you've ever been."

"You've known me for a week, Ryan Cody! Be quiet! God damn you." My angry, terrified whispered growl grew louder, but not really. He was teasing me for being loud when really it was a series of hushed, tight grumbles.

"Long enough to know that you're pretty brave when you want to be." He was so close I could feel his breath roll down my neck, sending a shiver over my spine. "Open your eyes, Rae."

"Absolutely not," I snapped at him, but he didn't budge from his pressed-up position on my side. His fingers curled around my chin, and I turned my face in his direction, his breath fanning over my cheeks.

"Look at me," Ryan's voice dropped to a stern tone, and it took everything in me to disobey him. "Lorraine Field, stop being a coward and look at me."

"I'm not a coward!" My eyes flew up and connected with his.

Evergreen danced with the twinkling lights of the ride, causing all the air in my lungs to rush out in a tiny, strangled gasp.

"There you are." He smiled, that stupid crooked and cocky smile that made my stomach do flips. He was so close to my face it was hard to focus on anything but him. The slope of his nose and the small smattering of freckles that danced across it, the redness to his cheeks. The way his lip twitched and gave away how nervous he really was. If it wasn't for how pretty Ryan was, I might have been sick to my stomach from my crippling fear.

"Why the hell do you love the Ferris wheel so much?" I asked him with a pathetic trembling lip, needing to understand the logic behind his enjoyment.

Ryan paused like he hadn't expected to be asked that. He wet his bottom lip, his eyes darting away for a second before looking back.

"Makes me feel untouchable," he said.

I nodded, trying to focus on his sudden, sad contemplation and not the heights.

"You're the most popular kid in school, baseball career. *You are untouchable,*" I said to him with a scoff.

Ryan sighed with a slight nod as his lips curled into a sad smile. "I know you saw more in that parking lot that day than you admitted to," he said. His shift in personality was jarring and concerning. "Baseball is a way out of that, being popular just—" he stopped. "I'm good at being funny and loud. I'm not so great at all the other stuff. I can swing a bat, run a base, flirt with a girl, but I can't focus in class. I can't put pen to paper."

I watched as he struggled to talk about his weaknesses but realized he was doing it to show that he was even afraid of the smallest situations.

"Up here, I don't have to be good at anything. I can just *be*." He explained. "Free of any pressure, I can breathe."

It was the most profound thing Ryan Cody had said to me in the week I had known him. We had more common ground than I cared to admit: the pressure to be the best, to reach for the stars as proxies for our parents. We were both suffocating under the weight of expectations in very different ways, but somehow, we were still the same.

"So, good at baseball, ladies man, but none of that matters in the eyes of my father. If I don't make something of myself, then I've failed everyone who believed me and pushed me to do that, and my Dad is just trying to make sure I stay on track." He swallowed, and I watched the cotton balls stick in his throat on the way down.

"With a firm hand?" I asked, finding my voice at quite possibly the worst time.

Ryan shrugged; the dismissal was unsettling. "A good crack to the head never hurt anyone," he said. When he looked back up at me, a fake smile was plastered on his face. "It's fine. It makes me remember what's important. It led me to you, " he said.

"That's an odd way to look at it. I'm not sure your Dad hitting you is kismet, Ryan."

"Well, I believe it was. Thinking straight gave me the chance to *see* you."

I stared at him momentarily, nervous to speak and say the wrong thing. With a thousand different options rolling around in my brain, there was a good chance I would anyway.

"*Great* at baseball," I said to him, his brows furrowed. "You said, *good,* but you're great at baseball."

"Alright," he laughed with a nod, the laugh finally genuine again. "Back to your crippling fear of heights. Count to five and look," his head nodded to the side, and a few pieces of his hair kicked up in the breeze against the smooth curve of his neck.

"I hate you, Ryan Cody," I said between two shallow breaths.

"I love you too, Starlight," he chuckled.

I hated how easily he said those words, like they were a compliment or a scientific fact he had read in some textbook. How could he even understand feelings as intense and life-altering as love? He was ridiculous. "You missed the five count," he smiled softly as his hand left my chin, knuckles brushing over my jaw, and gently redirected my gaze to the football field.

The lights from our height twinkled and pulled in the night sky in the most beautiful way, creating a kaleidoscope of colors that illuminated the darkness. Everyone looked so tiny from this high, and I had braced for the nauseous feeling, but it never came. The breeze licked my hot cheeks and filled my lungs with fresh air. I felt free.

"You alright?" He asked softly from beside me after a few moments of quiet.

I nodded with a small smile. "It's not so bad."

"You feel it, don't you?" he asked, shimmying so he was pressed completely against me, his eyes on me instead of the lights.

"I can breathe," I whispered and turned to look at him. Our faces were so close that the tip of his nose brushed against mine as I focused back on him. "Why did you call me Starlight?" I asked him quietly.

"Cause that's where you belong," he said with conviction. "With the stars."

The response wasn't what I had been expecting, and I wasn't sure what to say to him. Ryan Cody confused every rational thought I had all at once. I wanted to be mad at him for dragging me onto the ride, but no matter how hard I tried to dig the feeling up from my subconscious, I couldn't seem to find it. The irritation, the frustration... it had all melted away, leaving only a flourishing curiosity to understand him.

"You're staring at me like I have two heads," his brows pinched tightly, and his signature smile flattened into a straight line. "What's going on in there?" He asked.

"Astrophysics," I mumbled, half joking, but it made him bark and throw his head back. His hat fell from his head, and the wind rustled through the dirty blonde strands wildly as he brought himself back and pressed his forehead against mine.

The strands of his hair tickled my face as his eyes darted to my lips and back to my terrified gaze. I must have looked so stupid, frozen still from his touch, unsure of what he might do next but willing to let him…

His chest filled slowly, and his hand lifted to push a few pieces of my hair behind my ear, never taking his eyes off my lips. The brave little girl in me was screaming for him to do it. It would be my first, and what a story it would be.

But my mind was stringing together a cautionary tale in fragments: *he's a flirt, he does this with all the girls, you aren't the only one,* and worst of all, *this is all a game to him.*

"Ryan," the panic seeped from me, slowly at first, but then became a tidal away of fear as he inched toward kissing me.

Our lips brushed, so close to contact when the ride kicked to life. I yelped, ducking against his chest and digging my fingers into his sweater. My reflexes kicked into overdrive as he sighed and rested his chin on the top of my head.

"It's over," he whispered to me and shifted backward to catch my gaze as the ride stopped again, and the metal bar popped free, letting us off. "You earned some cotton candy," he said, staying close behind me as I took the stairs off the platform to the grass.

My stomach heaved, and I swallowed the vomit that rose quickly before giving him a small nod. "I'm going to go to the bathroom," I said, backing toward the school, he stepped in line to follow, but I shook my head.

I needed a moment to clear my thoughts and breathe air that wasn't tangled with his intoxicating smell. I had almost just kissed him, I had almost just let him kiss me… *oh god.* Ryan stared at me for a moment. I could tell he was contemplating ignoring me and following anyway, but he nodded.

"I'll go find you some sugar." He smiled softly and flipped his hat back over his messy hair.

The main hall of the school was open for access to the bathrooms, and there was a small line to wait in, but it gave me time to sort through all the wild thoughts that had been brought on by Ryan. The way his fingers felt on my skin, and he stared at me like I was the only person in the entire world. It was terrifying and exhilarating.

But I couldn't stop thinking about the fact that all of this was contrived. It was pieced together by the school in the form of tutoring sessions and forced interactions. Did Ryan want to be around me, or was I just a silly little distraction?

I needed to ask him.

When I finally got inside, the last stall in the girls' bathroom was empty, and I was almost finished when the sounds of three pairs of feet flooded in the door.

"He's just messing around," the voice of senior Cadence Williams huffed over the sound of two other girls agreeing with her instantly. It could only be Georgia and Paisley. "I just don't understand what his game is, hanging around someone like Loner Lorraine?"

Well, that hurts.

I waited quietly in my stall, tucking my feet against the base and all but holding my breath so they didn't hear me.

"I heard it's a bet he and Landry made," Paisley's high-pitched, droning voice echoed over the door, followed by Georgia's stupid giggle.

"Sure, who can get in the loser's pants the fastest?" Cadence hissed. "She's probably so desperate for human attention she doesn't even notice he's screwing with her."

I curled my hands into my lap and put my head down, just praying for them to leave soon. Sitting in the school bathroom crying in my lap about a boy wasn't exactly my plan for the night. But everything they said made sense. Why would he actually mean what he said? There was more than enough evidence that high school boys were mean and manipulative.

Was he out there laughing at me with his friends? Laughing that I had almost given in after only a week of talk? I must have seemed so pathetic. A tight, disbelieving laugh fell from me.

"Did you hear that?" Paisley said.

"Who's in here?" Georgia asked next, her boots stomping on the dingy titled floor outside my door. "I bet you it's her, listening to us talking about how tragic she is. Did you hear that little loner Lorraine? Ryan is fucking with you."

A sickening chorus of high school bully laughter echoed around the bathroom as the main door opened and swung shut, leaving me alone momentarily. I couldn't help the tears as they flowed, rubbing my nose on my sleeve as it started to run.

After a moment, there was a soft knock on my door. "Lorraine?" The voice was quiet, sweet even. "Are you okay?" she asked.

Far from it.

I stiffened, whipping my cheeks and popping the latch to find Mary Cooper from third-period advanced biology staring back at me with her glassy brown eyes and round cheeks. "I'm sorry they said those things," she said as I stood to walk to the bathroom. "They can be really mean, but Cadence's home life sucks, and Georgia's mom is cheating on her dad with the baseball coach."

"What?" I huffed, pausing as I washed my hands and turned my head to look at her.

"Paisley pretends to be better than everyone, but she lives down by the train-yard with her grandma in a trailer," Mary said as if that answered my question. "I'm just saying they're only mean because they need an outlet."

"Was that supposed to make me feel better?" I asked with a sniffle.

"No, but it levels the playing field. They were wrong," she said, handing me a sheet of paper towel for my wet hands. "You aren't tragic. They just don't know how to be themselves without putting others down."

"You talk a lot," I said gently as she took the wet towel and threw it out for me.

"But I'm not wrong." She smiled. "Do you want a walk home? I don't know about you, but I'm sick of this fair... they ran out of hot dogs an hour in, and Chet is running the kissing booth."

"Chet Perkins?" I raised an eyebrow. The thought of his creepy bird lips sent a shiver down my spine.

"I can see by the haunting look on your face you've been a victim to his weird locker letters," she laughed, her smile so bright it lit up all the dark spaces that were swallowing me whole. "I only live a street over from you. Your house is bigger, but we have a nicer yard that backs onto the lake. No offense," she hooked her arm in mine and dragged me toward the door. "My Mama said that you were feeling better?" She asked me, and I was a bit taken aback. "She talks to your Mama at town hall. She likes to check in on you after—"

"I'm fine," I said quietly with the small shake of my head. I wished my Mom would talk to *me* about anything. "It was just a cold."

"Lying isn't a great way to start a friendship, you know." She scoffed. "Mama said the radiation was hard on your body. That's why you missed so much school before Christmas."

"Stop, please," I said in a tiny voice. I didn't want to talk about that. I didn't want to even think about it. It was over. That was gone. I was fine.

"I'm sorry, I've got a problem. My Mama calls it a waterfall and always threatens to build a dam if I don't shut up. I just talk and talk. No one is ever really listening, but I talk anyways."

I had never spoken to Mary Cooper in my life, but here she was, filling the spaces of doubt and fear with her sweet, funny voice and her incessant rambling.

She was shorter than me, her head bobbing next to my shoulder as we wandered through the dark hallways to the other side of the school. I waved hello to Mr. Waters, the night janitor, and he let us out through the front.

For a moment, I felt bad about leaving Ryan behind, but I wasn't sure how to approach the situation. On one hand, I foolishly wanted to believe his actions and words—that maybe in some insane plane of reality, he really did just *like* me. But the rational part of my thinking was strong, arming every point my heart seemed to bring to my attention. A lot of 'why?' echoed around inside of me. Why *me*? Why *now*?

Maybe I needed a reality check from people who knew him better than anyone. It had only been a week, so I couldn't say I knew him—not really. What I knew was what he had shown me... but what had that been?

His sadness.

I swallowed the bile that rose, "do you think maybe Ryan might actually like me?" I asked Mary out of the blue as we walked.

She looked up at me and smiled, "he's been in the library every day this week."

My brows furrowed at her response.

"When you're invisible it makes it easier to pay attention to everyone around you. I help the librarian put books away at lunch. Until last week, I've never seen him in the library, except that one time he and Landry streaked through it and were suspended for a week."

"They streaked through the library?" I laughed suddenly, the sound almost terrifying against the backdrop of all my other problems.

"Butt naked." She laughed, "I was surprised, Landry has a pretty nice ass."

"Mary Cooper!" I joined back into the chorus of laughter.

"I'm just saying." She shrugged. "You should talk to him," she told me after the silence seeped between us. "He might surprise you."

I nodded and looked up at the stars. 'Starlight' his voice hummed in the back of my mind.

Please don't break my heart, Ryan Cody.

FIELD

I sat at my desk the next afternoon, writing a letter to Ryan that explained why I couldn't tutor him any longer. It hadn't been an easy conclusion to come to, but after laying in bed staring at the ceiling all night, I realized I couldn't let him plague me like that.

Whether or not he was truthful or lying, I shouldn't be tangled up so tight by a boy who had bulldozed into my life with only a month left of school. I had plans to graduate, to move away, to experience life without the fears of my mother and the nagging of my father...somewhere far from the sounds of hospital beeping and feelings of needles poking my skin.

I couldn't let a boy destroy my hope of freedom, not when I had come so far.

I had also re-written the letter four times, but none of the words came out properly. I hadn't even gone to school today, avoiding him properly the best I could until I figured out how to tell him.

I was surprised he hadn't shown up yet, banging on my door for answers. That seemed like the thing Ryan would do most. So I sat silently, trying to figure out exactly how to tell him all my feelings. Considering we weren't even...anything to one another, it seemed stupid. *I can no longer continue to assist Mr. Cody in his tutoring.*

That sounded cold.

I have simply too much preparation to do for my exams and my school work, so I will no longer be able to help Ryan.

That sounded insensitive.

I hate that everyone stares at me when he's around, and there's never anywhere to hide.

I'm a massive coward.

There had been too many times before when everyone whispered, wanting to know why I had missed so much school and where I had gone. Mostly, the rumors were that I had gotten pregnant, and they sent me to a convent to purge me of my sins and have the baby in private. That one was hilarious.

But the rumors were just that, rumors.

I *had* been sick. They found a tumor in my lung.

But radiation was enough for me to go into remission and return to school after a month of recovery at home. Not to mention the multiple arguments between my parents over whether or not I should go back. Mom had wanted me to stay home, to finish my senior year from my bed...my cage. Dad suggested I go back, that the rumors of my absence had started to affect his re-election.

So I went back to school, and they went back to ignoring me.

But Ryan complicated everything. Tutoring him was one thing, having a crush on a boy like him... It was messy, to begin with, stupid. Even admitting that I had inklings of those feelings felt dangerous, but I couldn't help myself. Every time he smiled at me, I forgot about the tumor, I forgot about the hospitals and the fighting. I forgot that there was a chance everything came crashing back down.

Ryan made me feel high, and it was terrifying.

So I had to stop tutoring him. I needed to stop seeing him because if this was a game to him- I set the pen down and sighed, staring at the botched letters as my stomach grumbled.

I tried several times, but nothing came out, so I pushed the papers aside and wandered downstairs. I ate a bowl of pasta on the island alone because Mom and Dad were out of town being friendly with the Governor or something. I didn't really care.

The quiet was peaceful, giving me time to think through my decision and cement my reasoning for not entertaining this tutoring deal any longer. The school could get mad if they wanted, but ultimately, no one could force me to continue helping Ryan. He was practically halfway through his assignments anyway, so it's not like it mattered.

He didn't need me to help him at all. He just wanted to draw attention to himself.

I cleaned up my mess and grabbed a glass of water before making my way back to my room. I was trying to decide which movie to watch when I noticed a shadow moving under my closed door.

Someone was in my room...

I pressed my ear to the wood, scared it might be an intruder, but sighed when I heard his soft mumbling. I opened the door to him in time to see him crumble to the floor at the end of my bed.

"Ryan?" I said when he didn't look up from his hands. "How did you get in my room?" I asked him. His dark blue t-shirt was ripped around the collar, his arms wrapped around his torso, and his legs stretched across my carpet. I would get yelled at later for the streaks of mud his cowboy boots left.

"I climbed up," he grumbled, still not looking at me.

"Get out," I huffed, "what is wrong with you? You can't just climb into people's windows."

"Yeah... yeah, I'll go—I, uh, this was dumb." He pushed to get up off the floor and that's when I saw it, *the state of his face.*

A large misshapen bruise painted his freckled face, a tiny gash splitting his once-perfect skin in a mixture of angry red and dark maroon dried blood. I stepped forward, my heart betraying my mind and squeezing tightly at the sight of him.

"What happened?" I asked.

He groaned with every step he took toward the open window, and I knew there were more bruises concealed on his torso with each ginger movement.

"It doesn't matter," he shook his head, strands of hair sticking to his cut cheek. "It's obvious that you don't want me here, I just—"

"You just what?" I said, setting the glass of water on my table and getting closer to him as he stepped away awkwardly.

"I started walking and ended up here." He confessed, turning around to meet my eyes. His eyes were red, and it only made the green of his irises brighter, almost painful in a way. The bruise on his cheek spread across the base of his eye, and a few broken vessels spidered across the white.

"Sit down," I said, pointing to the chair at my desk.

Ryan hesitated for a moment, unsure of my change in tone, but when I snapped my fingers, he shuffled his way and slumped down into the chair. I left the bedroom and found the first aid kit under my bathroom sink, taking a short moment to catch my breath before running a cloth under some warm water and returning it to him.

"Did you mean this?" He asked, his shaky fingers holding onto one of the half-finished letters. I hadn't meant for him to see those, and I cursed under my breath at my ignorance. I shook my head and wandered over to him, setting down the bag.

"Head up," I tapped gently under his chin, and he listened. His eyes trained on me as I moved around and dug out some things from the kit. "This is going to sting," I said, dabbing a warm cloth to his cheek to clean away the dried blood.

His hand clenched around the scattered papers on the desk, but he never closed his eyes, even as his body tensed and his jaw tightened. Ryan continued to watch me.

"Are you going to tell me what happened?" I asked him again.

"It doesn't matter. I'll leave when you're done. I won't bug you anymore." He said in a string of careful, tight words.

"Ryan," I said, but he stopped me, his fingers wrapping around my wrist, pushing my hand away from his face so he could stand up.

He hovered over me, his hands at his side and his eyes rolling over my face. "What did I do?"

The question caught me off guard. Maybe I had expected him to defend himself or make excuses, but even after reading the fragments of letters I never finished, he still didn't know. Or maybe he just didn't understand because I was wrong.

"I meant everything I said, Rae." His bottom lip shook, and I noticed another small bruise forming around the corner. "I just don't know what happened in between..."

The Ferris wheel and tonight.

"Alright, stop, just for a second." I put my hands up, "I want to know what happened to you before anything else."

Ryan ran a hand through his hair, followed by a strangled whimper as his body stretched awkwardly. I wanted to know how bad it was but wasn't brave enough to ask. My eyes flickered back up to his, and he was still watching me nervously. And it was only when he looked away that confirmed there was more damage he was concealing.

"After you didn't come out of the bathroom, I knew I had screwed something up, so I went and got drunk with Landry. It was stupid, but I was—" he stopped and shook his head, "I was sad." He said. "I didn't know what I did, but I knew you were mad at me. There's no way you'd just vanish like that. And then I sat in the library all morning knowing you had a free period before lunch, but you never came in."

"I stayed out sick," I said quietly.

"I know," he said in a stuttered voice, "I know that now. I skipped my afternoon classes cause I was mad at you and myself for not trying harder. I was pissed off and confused, so I went home, and my Dad found out," he said. "We got in a fight."

"A fight?" I said, my brows coming together in disbelief, "or a beating?" I asked him.

He looked at me for a long moment, his eyes so dark I could barely tell they were green. "It doesn't matter. I walked away, and I walked until I ended up on your lawn without thinking."

"You were mad at me?" I scoffed.

"Yeah, I was, Rae!" Ryan said with conviction, "no matter what I do to show you I love you, you don't believe me!" He argued.

"You can't love someone after seven days, Ryan!" I said. "And because that's true, it means you're playing games with me! Everyone sees it! Cadence—"

"That's why you took off? Cadence, Georgia, and Paisley? Those girls are nothing but rude, cruel chickens, pecking and clucking, and if that's not where you were going with that sentence, I don't wanna hear it, Rae. They hold no weight in this conversation. *It's you and me.*"

The tone of his voice was more serious than I had ever heard him be.

"I love you, Lorraine Field. I knew it the second you turned those angry, terrified, blue eyes on me that day. I believe it, and every day you don't breaks my heart a little more! I am going to run out of glue trying to put it back together." His hands grabbed my face, his jaw ticking in pain from the movement. "Why do you listen to everyone else's noise but you never wanna listen to me?"

"I'm scared," I said to him, and his features softened with a shaky exhale. "You scare me."

CODY

"That's life, Rae!" I said to her when she said that she was scared if that was her only reason for running away. "Being scared is a part of life," I lowered my voice.

My head was pounding, and the cut on my cheek stung so badly it kept making my eyes water. Dad had never gotten *that* mad. It wasn't exactly unwarranted. I had shown up back home in a huff, pissed off at myself, pissed off at Lorraine. I was confused, sad, heartbroken.

In a matter of a week, a girl upended my entire world, and while I saw an opportunity to feel something off the field, Dad wasn't as enthusiastic about my new *fixation*.

That's what he had called her, a fucking fixation. Like she wasn't the brightest star in the entire sky, as if I wasn't meant to spin around in her gravity for the rest of my life. In that moment, all the frustration with Lorraine melted away, and it bubbled up in anger toward my Dad for talking about her like that.

Next thing I knew, we were throwing punches, Riona was screaming for Dad to stop and my oldest brother, Robert, was trying to rip us apart. Dad told me to get gone, go I did.

All the way here.

"I don't want to be scared!" She argued, pulling me from my own head back into her room. I shouldn't even be here. In her room like this. *Idiot*.

"Too bad!" I said, throwing my arms up. "Too fucking bad!" I repeated, watching her flinch as I swore. "I love you, and I know you think that's stupid, but I've been telling you since the day we met, and I'll be telling you that until the day we die."

"You've known me—"

I cut her off, "a week, yeah, I know. You keep using that as an excuse. You aren't a game to me. This isn't a bet I made with Landry," I said and her eyebrows raised. "Yeah, I hear them whisper too, but you know what? I don't listen to them. Everything they say is to make themselves feel better and it has nothing to do with what happens with us."

The devastatingly sad look in her glassy blue eyes burrowed down into my chest.

"They called me *Loner Lorraine*," she said quietly, and I knew where this was going. "Just like you call Carlos, kooky."

"I never called you that, not once," I argued.

"But you're friends with the people that do, who see me in that light. You want this epic love story so badly you aren't stopping to look at the facts!" Lorraine shook her head, "people like us aren't meant to be together."

"That's bullshit," I said with a shrug, "I told you on the ride how I felt about being popular, that it's just a show for everyone else. But with you, I'm just me. I don't have to be funny or loud. You just... it sounds stupid when I say it out loud but you make me wanna sit in the quiet with you."

She huffed, but I watched the corners of her mouth upturn into a small smile. "I know you're scared," I said to her. "I'm scared too, but you were scared of the Ferris wheel, and you still got on it for me?"

Lorraine peered up at me through thick lashes and inhaled slowly. I watched her chest rise and fall softly as she reasoned with her inner thoughts. I held mine, terrified that she would still send me away even after all this. I'd have to go sleep on one of Landry's pool chairs in the backyard because going home wasn't an option at the moment.

"Because you asked me to, because you—" she stopped, clearly frustrated with me.

"I held your hand, I asked?" I laughed. "I'm asking you right now to do the same thing," I said. "Hold my hand, don't shut me out."

The storm in her eyes raged as she tried to work through everything. Still very conflicted about everything that I had said to her, I just had to wait and hope that she believed me—or at least that I could get to a place where she could *start* to believe me.

"Are you hungry?" She asked me suddenly, after all that silence, that's what she asked me, and I started to laugh.

"I'm starving," I admitted, my breath hitching when she extended her hand to me, fingers softly wiggling. I took it without question, my knuckles sore from the fight, but I didn't care because the moment our palms connected, her warm touch soothed every ache.

Their house was twice the size of mine, and it was a wonder she didn't get lost as we wandered down the hall and toward the stairs.

"Your parents won't be mad," I asked her as we headed toward the main floor.

She shook her head, "they're gone for the week."

"You're alone in this house for a week?" I said, my tone shocked because she looked at me in confusion over her shoulder. "How often do they leave you alone like that?" I asked her.

"All the time, there are housekeepers around..." she tugged me into the kitchen and pointed to one of the stools at the massive island. The kitchen alone was bigger than the main floor of my house, with dark wood cabinets and fancy countertops that didn't look plastic. She dug in the drawers and pulled out some forks before going into the fridge.

She balanced a small, half-eaten cake in one hand and two sodas in the other. I reached forward and helped her despite the groan of my sore ribcage. It was vanilla with pink frosting. It looked like she had been picking at it all night, and the scribbled white font on the top was half gone, but I could tell that it was her birthday cake.

"When was your birthday?" I asked her with a pit in my stomach.

"It's tomorrow," she said with a shrug like it wasn't a big deal.

"Rae." I stopped her from moving away from the island with my hand on her wrist, "it's your birthday tomorrow?"

"Yeah, just like it was last year and the year before."

"Were you going to celebrate alone?" I asked her and pinned my shoulders back, looking around at her big empty house, suddenly mad at everyone in her life.

"It's just a birthday, Ryan," She said to me and handed me a fork.

"It's *your* birthday," I argued against her blatant lack of concern. If she wasn't going to be angry, I would be angry for her. "You should never be alone on your birthday."

"I'm an only child," Lorraine said, taking a bite of cake.

"That makes it worse! I have six siblings, and my Mom remembers every single one of our birthdays. If anything, she should be forgetting one or two a year," I laughed. "They only have you to celebrate, and they're not even home."

"It's fine, I'm used to it. They left me presents, and I baked myself a cake." She smiled down at it.

"You baked that yourself?" I said in shock as the vanilla sponge cake melted in my mouth. She smiled at me, "It's really good but that's also really sad."

"Thank you," she said, unscrewing the soda cap from the corner of her shirt and handing it to me before doing her own. "You know my parents may leave me alone, but at least they don't hit me."

I laughed hard, mostly because I didn't know how else to interpret her statement. "Yeah, I guess you're right." I shook my head. "I kind of earned it this time."

"Ryan, you're a child; you don't *earn* beatings," She said quietly, "You might be the most insufferable person in this town, but he's still your dad."

"I'll be out of there soon enough," he said.

"If you finish your papers," she reminded me.

"My tutor quit," I looked at her with a smile.

"Tried to," she laughed, and the sound created a burst of fireworks across my chest.

"Please don't, I need your help," I said.

"No, you don't. Half of those assignments you've done on your own. You're just trying to impress me." Lorraine sipped on her soda. "The other half you don't want to do because you're *scared*."

"Hey now," I took another bite of cake.

"It's true. It just wasn't clear before. You don't want to do any of the papers that involve any sort of childhood memory or family members. You avoid them." She said it as if it was a matter of fact.

And maybe it was.

"I didn't come over here for a therapy session, Starlight." I hummed as a joke, but the darker reasonings of my impromptu visit tonight. I hated that she saw through my defenses and always found me hiding in some dark corner of my mind.

"Right, you just came for the cake." She held up a spoonful. "You can sleep in the guest room tonight," she offered. "But you have to take those boots off. If you get mud anywhere else, my Mom will kill me."

I looked down at my boots, hand-me-downs from my brother Robert. They fit funny around my ankles, but they did the job. My mind completely glazed over the fact that she said I could stay here.

"Did you say I could stay?" I looked back up at her, and she nodded.

"Where else are you going to go?" Her little laugh was a breath of fresh air.

"I would have gone to sleep at Landry's," I said honestly, and she scrunched her nose up at me. "But I'd rather stay here."

Lorraine stared at me for a long moment, the silence stretching out tight until finally, she smiled at me, and it broke with a snap. God, I loved her. It was stupid and it hurt, but it was the truth, even if she wasn't ready for it.

"Alright, I'll find you some clean clothes." She said with a tiny sigh. "Stay put."

"Yes, ma'am," I nodded and went back to eating cake.

The rest of the night was spent sitting on the floor of the guest room with me while she showed me all her constellation books. She had drawn everything by hand and left cute little descriptions in the margins of each star she liked.

It was like holding a piece of her in my hands, and I treasured it.

I was still stuck on the idea that her birthday was tomorrow, and she hadn't said anything. In fact, if I hadn't gotten in the fight with my Dad, she would have been left to sit alone in this massive cold house.

Tomorrow, I'd wake up and make everything perfect for her.

She looked over at me with a soft smile to make sure I was still paying attention to her rambling about the stars, making my heart race. *I owe her the perfect day.*

FIELD

"Morning, Starlight," Ryan said as I wandered into the kitchen in my pajamas.

My toes still tingled as my body started to wake from sleep. I tucked my fingers into the pocket of my hoodie to keep them warm. My hair was tugged messily into a ponytail, and I was still rubbing the sleep from my eyes as I took in the kitchen.

"Ryan..." I said, unable to help the laughter that tumbled from me. "What are you doing?"

"Making you breakfast?" He said, his words curling up in confusion at the end as he turned to look at me. "Don't tell me you don't like pancakes," he sighed and looked over at the towering plate.

"I love waffles," I laughed and leaned against the island. "I'm just not sure I can eat *that* many."

Ryan pouted, a full-on bottom-lip pout, as he looked over at me before saying, "Coward," as a smirk grew on his face.

"Did you just call me a coward? You made like fifteen pancakes," I pointed to the plate where he stacked another one. I can maybe eat two," I said as my stomach grumbled. "Okay, maybe three," I added, which brought his smirk into a full-blown smile.

I watched as he wandered back and forth, making me a plate. Everything he did was purposeful, and his brows were scrunched in concentration as he moved. When he was finally satisfied, he nodded to himself and set the plate down in front of me, beaming with pride.

Moving around me, I sucked in a tiny breath as he wrapped his arms around my shoulders and leaned over me. His lips close to my ear as he pressed our bodies together. He had cut up strawberries and bananas, scattering the plate with them before he slathered everything in whipped cream.

"Happy birthday, Rae." He whispered to me and handed me a fork.

"You know you didn't have to do this. I really wasn't upset about it," I said to him. And that was the honest-to-God truth. Birthdays held no sentimental value to me. We never really celebrated anyone's birthday in our house. It wasn't just me. To my family, it was just another day on the calendar that could be crammed with meetings, chores, and educational activities.

But my heart was racing at an uncomfortable speed as Ryan waited for me to take a bite. He was so proud of himself for making such a nice breakfast. It was endearing, and I couldn't find the proper words to convey how grateful I was for his gesture.

I cupped my hand over the overflowing fork and lifted it to my lips. Everything melted together, and it actually tasted really good. I turned my head not thinking about his proximity, only wanting to praise his cooking skills, and found his face millimeters from mine.

Time wasn't relevant. Everything seemed to slow down, and each detail of his face became glaringly obvious. The way his throat bobbed, the sparkle in his eyes as the gold danced across the green, and how bold the color was framed by the nasty purple bruise on his face. But distractingly so, and the worst of all was the small, nervous smirk on his lips. Our nose brushed together, and for a second, I thought he would pull away, but he only nuzzled closer.

"These are really good pancakes," I whispered to him, uncomfortably confessing the compliment to distract me from my nervousness.

"It's the only thing I can make, don't be too impressed." He huffed, and his breath warmed my skin.

Ryan's eyes flickered to my lips as I cleaned the whipped cream from my bottom lip, and his entire body groaned, leaning forward to close the space even further.

"I would like to kiss you," he said quietly, "but only if—"

SO LONG, HONEY

I didn't let him finish the sentence. I pushed my chin toward him and closed the little space between our lips. Kissing him without hesitation as my heart thudded wildly in my chest, and the crescendo of time seemed to stop altogether. His hands tangled into my hair, curling around my jaw to pull me impossibly close. The kiss itself was soft and careful. His bottom lip captured mine and sent a burst of fireworks across my chest. My skin tingled with heat from his touch.

When he pulled away, I felt my body follow him, only for a soft laugh to tumble from his lips as he pressed another short kiss to mine. "I didn't think it was possible to love you more."

I rolled my eyes at his ridiculousness, but instead, I was a ball of nerves. *Did he like it? Was it okay?* I had never kissed a boy before, and now... "if you hated that, I'm never going to celebrate my birthday ever again in my entire life." My cheeks flushed.

"Rae," Ryan wrapped his hands around my face. "You are perfect." His words held conviction. To be so sure of everything he did and said must have been a wild feeling. One I couldn't relate with, I was intelligent and quick with my words, but I had never met a person so aware of their strengths the way Ryan Cody was.

"Now eat," he instructed. "I want you to show me what you usually do on your birthday so we can do something better."

I scoffed at his teasing and turned back to my pancakes, only for him to stick his finger into the pile of whipped cream. Then he popped the cream-covered finger into his mouth with a smile so bright it made me feel like I was staring at the sun.

"Thank you for sticking your dirty fingers in my breakfast," I laughed with a tiny shake of my head. As I ate, Ryan moved around to clean up the mess he had made, much to my surprise. I had expected to have to do it later before my parents got home. By the time I was finished, he was leaning against the counter with a pancake and a can of whipped cream.

"Watch this," he laughed as he folded the pancake up like a taco and loaded it full of whipped cream before shoving it in his mouth.

"That was disgusting," I watched him in bewilderment.

"You're impressed, don't lie." Ryan smiled with full cheeks and a little wink that made my stomach do flips. "Go get dressed," he said, leaning over the island and taking my plate.

I watched him for a moment before listening to him and finding my way upstairs. I pulled on a pair of jeans and a T-shirt with a sweater that covered my arms. I looked down at my skin. There were a few new random purple bruises that I didn't remember where they had come from. I scowled at them before tugging the sweater on and going to find Ryan.

He was slipping into his boots as I rounded the stairs to the front entrance, his hair falling messily in his face and his breathing labored.

"Are your ribs still bothering you?" I asked him as he straightened out and huffed a shaky breath with a small nod. "You should go get them looked at today," I suggested.

"They'll heal." He shrugged and reached over to push a piece of rogue hair behind my ear. I swear, every time he touched me, my body flooded with heat. "Where first, Starlight?"

I thought about my last birthday and smiled, "do you trust me?" I asked him.

"I'd follow that mischievous smile over a cliff," he responded without hesitation and extended his hand to me, wiggling his fingers.

We walked down through the gate into town after leaving my house. Ryan never strayed too far, and even as we reached Main Street, he never let go of my hand. Even when a few girls from class passed us, even as he waved and talked to some people in town, he held tight.

"In here," I said to him as we reached the tiny shop.

Ryan's eyes doubled in size as we wandered inside. The shop was lined with shelves, jam-packed with little glass and ceramic nicknacks that the world had deemed ugly or useless, all sitting here waiting to be loved.

Mrs. Bates was behind the counter, her wild blonde hair puffed up on top of her head, adding at least a foot of extra height to her tiny five-foot frame. She had always been a little scary, with pale skin and the voice of a lifetime smoker. It was a wonder she was even still alive, let alone running the shop by herself.

"Morning, Mrs. Bates," I said to her in passing and she grumbled something under her breath. "This is Ryan," I told her, even though she didn't care to hear it. "Come on, the best part is over here." I dragged him toward the left front window.

The display had never changed, and if she ever found the energy to do so, I'd probably cry because a bundle of glass sun catches hung from every possible hook. There had to be at least thirty of them, all catching the sun in the bay window that looked out onto main street. The sun peered through them, creating a confetti rainbow across the floor and walls.

Ryan watched me with curiosity, letting me spin in a circle and moving without effort to continue to hold my hand. His eyes roamed the walls and floors, landing on the collection of suncatchers with a smile.

"It's incredible," he said, "I didn't even know this store existed."

"Most don't," I shrugged. There's something about it that makes me so happy—all these lost treasures, just begging to be found."

Ryan stared at the side of my face as I turned to look at the hundreds of trinkets before me. Something about being lost in the store, with all the other forgotten pieces of art, soothed my soul and made me feel at home.

"Pick one out," he said, and my head whipped to him.

"No, I just look," I said to him, That was enough for me.

"Rae, pick one," He insisted. "Or I'll pick the ugliest one in the shop and give it to you as a present." He teased, his fingers digging into my side and making me giggle.

"Be careful!" Mrs. Bates' froggy rasp echoed over the shop louder than I had ever heard her speak. "You break it, you buy it." She slapped a sign that hung behind her on the wall with her cane, nearly hitting ten glass objects as she did.

"Okay, okay." I pushed his fingers away from my ribs with a tiny huff. I wasn't used to such affection, and it was overwhelming—like an adrenaline rush every time he touched me. After a good twenty minutes of wandering around, I finally found a tiny glass sculpture of an angel holding a moon. It was no bigger than a palm, but she was made of the prettiest light purple glass with flecks of white and blue throughout.

"That one," I pointed to it, and Ryan gently picked it up and paid for it, handing me the small brown bag with a smile. "Thank you," I said to him, and he smiled down at me, creeping forward with his hand still on the bag, too. He tugged me toward his chest until he was within reach to kiss me.

In public.

I inhaled a shaky breath as he pulled away.

"Are you okay?" He asked in a hushed voice, but all I could do was nod. "Are you sure?"

"Yeah, I just didn't expect you to…"

"Kiss you?" Ryan's brows furrowed, "Rae…" He leaned close and kissed me again, "Now that I've done it once, I'll need them at least once an hour until the day we die."

I stared up at him, my heart racing so fast it felt like it would burst out of my chest on main street. "I mean in public."

"Am I not allowed to kiss you in public?" He asked quietly, matching my tone.

"I—well…" I shrugged; I had just expected him to.

"If I ever gave you the idea that I was ashamed to be seen with you, Starlight, you're going to have to remind me when because I'm blanking." Ryan smiled down at me because he was right. Never once had he pretended like I wasn't there around anyone. It had been him who wanted to sit in the library for our tutoring, him who dragged me to the fair…

"I'm sorry. I guess it was just a surprise," I said.

Ryan kissed me again, and it warranted the same rush of heat as before.

"I'll kiss you until you're comfortable, I'll kiss you until the whole town knows it." He declared, "I'll even scream it down the street. *I kissed Lorraine Field!*" He said a little louder.

"Ryan, don't you dare!" I laughed and pulled him back for a third kiss before he could act on the foolish notion. He smiled against my mouth and pressed his fingers to my throat, holding me in place as he leaned his weight over me and deepened the kiss.

"What's next?" He asked when he finally pulled away.

"You said you wanted to see the bowling queen in action?" I smirked up at him.

"Oh, God. I've never wanted anything more," He laughed and tossed his arm over my shoulder as we started down the street toward the alley.

CODY

"Here," I knelt in front of her on the bench, despite the deep pain in my side, and tied the laces of her bowling shoes for her. When I looked up to see if they were too tight, she stared down at me with the stars in her big blue eyes.

The lights from the dark bowling alley reflected back at me, paired with her big smile, was enough to drive a boy over the edge of insanity. It had been such a short time, but I couldn't remember a moment without her now. She consumed all my thoughts, to the point that until this very moment, I had stopped to think about my Dad or baseball.

I just didn't care about any of it when I was around her. It was terrifying and exhilarating all at once. I knew full well that baseball needed to be focused on. It was my ticket out, and now I had another person to take with me.

I'd be damned if I left her behind in a town that doesn't see her light.

I needed to work hard, finish my papers, and practice more. I had a newly formed responsibility to her and myself. To be the best I could.

"You're going to start to smoke if you think any harder." She said, her fingers brushing under my chin to hold my gaze.

"Lost myself for a second. Luckily, I have the North Star sitting in front of me." I beamed at her and stood up from the floor. "Come on, show me those skills."

She took my hand in her own, never saying a word, but her cheeks blushed deep pink, and she tucked in close as we navigated the busy bowling alley. There were tons of kids here today, a few families, but mostly the senior crowd that liked to waste Saturday afternoons gossiping.

"We're number nineteen," I said to her, and she weaved around a group of old ladies sipping coffee to find our alley. "Do you need the bumpers up to score your perfect game?"

"Do you?" Lorraine countered as she set her shoes and bag on the cushioned pinstripe bench.

"You're cocky, Starlight. This won't end well." I teased her.

"You may be good at baseball, Cody, but you can't cheat math." She ran her eyes over me with a smirk and took her turn first. "Watch closely now. Maybe you'll learn something."

I laughed loudly and leaned back against the bench to watch her score a perfect strike. Her small hands commanded the bowling ball, and with a simple side step, she bent her knee and sent the ball down the lane toward the pins for a strike.

I sat up and clapped for her slowly, "alright that was pretty impressive."

"Afraid to lose?" She asked me. Strands of her dark hair fell around her face, and her smile was infectious.

Mirroring the look on her face, I stood up, "for the first time in my entire life, no. I'm not." I said to her because it didn't matter if she kicked my ass at bowling, she could do it every day for the rest of our lives, and I'd lose every time, fair and square, if it meant I got to see that smile.

"Show me what you got," she spun away from me and plopped down to the bench with her body leaning toward me, her hands cupped against the fabric to hold her steady as I chose a ball. "They're all the same."

"No, no," I hushed her playfully. "They aren't; they give off auras." I teased as my lips pulled into a smirk.

"You're mocking my play style, I see you," Lorraine giggled with a roll of her eyes.

"I would never," I commented, stopping my hand with a funny gasp as I reached a dark blue ball with green flecks. "This is the one," I said to her, my heart racing.

"How do you know?" She asked with so much curiosity in her eyes.

"I just do," I said with conviction.

Her shoulders were tense for a hair longer before she finally took a breath and relaxed, it was apparent that she still wasn't completely convinced with my decision. I could see the doubt flicker around her face but just as soon as it had appeared, it was gone again. I was slowly finding my way through her defenses to the darker corners of who she was and who she could be.

I stepped up to the line, dropped the ball to my side, unaware of how heavy it was, and grunted. "How do you even throw these things?" I gaped at her, but all she did was shrug.

I tried to ignore how it felt to have her eyes on my back as I attempted to prove her math theory wrong. Swinging my arm back, I stepped forward, and as soon as I let the ball go, I knew I'd never hear the end of it. The ball bounced awkwardly before rolling into the gutter.

"You get three," was all she said when I turned around to face her.

"Uh, huh." I shook my head and took the second ball. I could tell she wanted to give me pointers, but she kept her mouth closed and let me flounder.

After another gutterball I finally managed to actually throw the ball straight, knocking over two whole pins.

"I guess you're better at catching," she teased from the bench.

"I'm warming up." I shrugged. "Are you hungry?" I asked her, and she nodded gently. " Soda?" I added.

"Please," her voice was quiet as I leaned over her, trapping her on the bench with my arms as I kissed her slowly, right there in the middle of all that chaos. Her body was tense at first but slowly relaxed under my touch. "Breathe, Starlight. No one cares about two teenagers making out in a bowling alley," I told her as I stole another kiss and backed away to grab her snacks.

Leaving her there, I pushed past a few crowds to the counter and waited to be noticed. Carson, our center fielder, nodded at me and excused himself to come help me. His fiery red hair and abnormally sized blue eyes paired terribly with the pinstripe bowling uniform.

"What's up, Cody?" He said with that dragged-out drawl of his.

"I just need some sodas and popcorn." I pointed to the board, and he nodded.

"Since when does Cadence drink soda?" He laughed while pouring the drink.

"I'm not here with Cadence," I shook my head and looked around, trying to get a look at Lorraine, but the crowd had shifted and my line of sight to her was closed off. I tapped my fingers on the counter impatiently, desperate to get back to her. I laughed at myself, so foolishly attached and so fast. But it only bothered me when I thought about it. When I told *myself* how foolish I was being, every other moment with Lorraine was an adventure. It wasn't too fast or too soon. It was just right. It felt right to be that in love with her in that moment and everyone else could think what they wanted.

All I wanted was her.

"Who are you here with then? Paisley?" He asked, setting down the cups. "I hear she—"

"Carson, don't finish that sentence," I said as he slid the popcorn across the counter. "I'm here with Lorraine Field."

"Loner Lorraine?" He laughed, and I cocked my head to give him a dirty look. "Sorry, yeah, that was dumb, it just—"

"It's just what?" I growled as I leaned over the counter and grabbed a package of candy. "You'll cover this for me, right?" I waved it in the air at him with a smile that screamed, *"If you ever talk about her like that again, I'll do more than steal candy.* "

"Yeah, man, on the house."

"Good, thanks, Carson. I'll see you tomorrow at practice." I said scooping everything into my arms and walking back to Lorraine. She was exactly where I left her, but something was wrong. She looked pale, and her hands were gripping the bench to get her upright. I slid everything on the table and knelt in front of her.

"Rae, you okay?" I asked her, and she nodded, but I could tell it was just her brushing me off. "What can I do?"

"Nothing. I'm just a little dizzy," she said quietly, inhaling a slow, methodical breath.

"You have to breathe out," I said to her when she didn't, and a little chuckle fell from her lips as she released a shaky exhale. "Good, do that again."

She listened, slowly filling her lungs before exhaling all the air. After a tortuous few minutes, the color finally returned to her face and she opened her eyes to look at me.

"What happened?" I asked her, reaching for the soda to give to her. She wrapped her lips around the straw instead of answering me and sipped on the dark, sugary liquid.

"I just stood up too fast, is all," she confessed, "I'm alright, I think I was just hungry."

I watched her and tried to gauge whether she was actually telling me the truth, but I couldn't tell. She was too good at hiding what she was really thinking.

"I bowled another strike while you were gone," she chuckled weakly as I tried to find my bearings on the situation.

"Of course you did." I shook my head and looked at the scorecard. "Are you sure that you're okay?"

"Stop ruining my birthday with your worrying," she responded.

"Says that girl who didn't even want to celebrate her birthday today," I laughed. "After this game, I'm taking you home. It's the end of the story."

Lorraine nodded in agreement, but something was missing that had been there before... a light that had been snuffed out. I left her where she was sitting to take my turn, and all three of my balls went in their own direction, hitting one pin each and doing nothing for my score.

"I can throw a ball at fifty miles per hour, can't make a bowling ball go in a straight line..." I said as I sauntered back to her.

"Bowling isn't baseball. Maybe that's why you're so bad at it." She shrugged gently and pushed from her seat on shaky knees.

I watched every move she made with concern. It was clear she was hiding something, that much I had figured out, but the 'what' was making my heart race faster than it ever had, and I wasn't sure I could go much longer without plying her with questions she probably didn't want to answer.

"You need to separate your feet and not force the ball to where you want it to go. It's a soft and powerful swing, not an aggressive one, " she explained with a small smile. "Like this."

I watched her struggle to carry the weight of the ball without a small stumble in her step, but when she lined herself up for the throw, it was like watching the wind. Her movements were soft and gentle. It wasn't like she was throwing a ball. It was like she was guiding it. Her hair licked at her neck, and her smile bloomed wide as all the pins crashed around, and she scored another strike. She turned to me proudly and arched her brow at me in a cute but cocky way that I had never expected from her.

"Rae, that was the hottest thing ever." I held my hands up in the air and admitted defeat. "You really are the bowling Queen of the Wild West." I mocked a bow, tempted to get on my knees and sell it, but she rushed forward to make me stop in a fit of laughter.

"They're staring again. Stop it," she giggled. When she leaned back away from me to catch her breath, my lips found the base of her throat. Her skin was colder than before but heated up on contact as she melted into me.

"I like it when they stare," I whispered to her.

"Of course you do; you thrive on attention." She scoffed, but she let me kiss her anyway.

Lorraine ended up winning the game. I hadn't stood a chance against her skills.

Even wobbly and maybe even dizzy, she nailed every ball she threw. It was infuriating.

"Rematch next weekend." I smiled at her as we left the bowling alley.

"Deal," she cooed and slid her hand into mine.

FIELD

"Rae," Ryan's fingers wrapped around my wrist as I climbed the steps to my house. Today was fun but tiring, and all of my muscles were aching. I knew he was a ticking time bomb of questions just from how he looked at me from the bottom of the stairs.

"Thank you for today. I don't think I've had this much fun on my birthday ever," I said, leaning into his touch.

"Are you sure you're okay?" He asked again. He had asked twice while we were finishing bowling and on the walk home. "I'd hate for you to be sick and leave you. You need like soup or something, I can go-"

"Ryan," I said to him, my voice pulling his attention back. His eyes are so big and hopeful that it nearly breaks my heart. Suddenly, the world doesn't feel so big again, it's back to just us, and I feel safe enough for a split second to say something stupid. "Soup won't fix this."

"Soup can fix anything," he said, not quite catching on to the severe tone of my voice.

"No..." I said. I turned to look at him and almost lied, telling him it was just a headache or something that didn't feel so daunting in my mind. His brows scrunched together in confusion, waiting for more and clearly concerned.

"Last year, I was gone for a while," I mumbled, unable to find my voice.

Ryan closed the space between us. "You're making me nervous, Starlight," he said.

"Will you sit, please." I pleaded with him when he froze, watching me.

"I remember, not *you* exactly," he said with a sad voice and lowered to the steps beside me, "but everyone talking about the mayor's daughter just being *gone.*"

"I was diagnosed with leukemia, Ryan." I said to him, "I went away because I had to spend five days in a hospital for radiation…" I trailed off, trying not to cry. Everything surrounding that year felt like someone settling weights on my chest, piling and piling until I couldn't bear it any longer. "I was a mess, dizzy, sick all the time."

"Dizzy like today?" Ryan sat forward, his jaw tight like he was assembling the messed up puzzle of my life with half the pieces missing.

"I'm in remission, it—" I tried to explain to him without causing more panic but that was pointless as he had already gone over the edge.

"So the cancer is gone?" His voice was brimming with hope, and it broke my heart as his fingers tangled with mine and rested them on his lap. I wanted to tell him yes, that it was gone, that I was cured, but I couldn't lie to him. Not after how honest he had been all day, not with how scared he looked now.

"No, well, sort of…" I said quietly, "There's no cure for it, just treatment and prayers." I scowled at the last bit. I could see him processing the information slower than I would have wished, but he wasn't flipping out. It was a decent start. He was now part of the *Lorraine might be dying club*. If only it counted toward community service hours, it might help him get into college.

The part I hated the most about when my parents found out was the look on their faces. Never once had I seen compassion or fear from them, but in that moment, it was all they showed. It was like feeling sorry would make it all better.

"That must have been terrifying," he whispered. "I'm sorry."

"It's life, Ryan," I said quietly. "Bad things happen to good people."

"Nothing bad should ever happen to you." Ryan shook his head, arguing a simple fact of life like he could change the saying. He was quiet for a long time, probably unsure of what to say to me, and understandably so. The girl he supposedly loved had just told him she was diagnosed with a cancer that could rear its ugly head whenever it felt like it.

"The radiation did its job, and when I got the chance to come home, I wanted to go right back to school, but my parents argued over it for a long time, so I spent some time here, alone until I was strong enough to go back to school but by then…"

"Everyone had told just about every nasty rumor they could think of, " he finished for me with a subtle nod. "You did all of that by yourself?" His comment caught me off guard. I had expected more piling about the leukemia or the treatment, but he was asking about *me*.

"My parents were around," I said.

"Like they were today?" He countered, and he was right. Even in the city, Dad was always in meetings, and Mom would show up for a few minutes every morning to bring me fresh flowers, homework, and clean pajamas. But it had been mostly spent alone.

"There was this nice nurse, Kelly. She had this laugh that got high-pitched when I made a really funny joke," I said to him, but Ryan didn't laugh. He barely smiled. "I'm alright now. We do tests to check every six months, and today was the first time I'd gotten dizzy. I'm sure it was just because I hadn't eaten in a while. My appetite is still a little wonky from everything." I said, aware of my rambling but nervous that he would get scared or leave.

He was only seventeen, after all. My parents had handled all the news worse.

"I thought cancer was supposed to make all your hair fall out?" He reached forward and brushed his fingers over a strand of my hair.

"It's a wig," I said to him. "I have a few. They were presents from my mom to make me feel more *normal*."

Ryan stared at the strand between his fingers, "it feels so real," he whispered.

"It should. They were a lot of money. I get told once a week." I said. "My hair is coming back, but…"

"Show me," he blurted, but it was soft and whispery in the warm air.

"I don't—" I chewed on my lip. I barely ever left my room without them on. When Mom had first given me one, I had been angry, pissed off that she was trying to cover up the sickness, but over time, they had become a safety blanket for me. I couldn't imagine how the kids would look at me at school if they had seen my patchy growth months ago.

"Rae, I'm not going to find you less beautiful without some hair," he smiled at me with encouragement in his eyes.

He said that now...

"Please." The sound of his voice broke through my nerves and landed true. I inhaled slowly, filling my lungs with a long, shaky breath before I tugged the wig from my scalp. A few barrettes and pins popped as I did.

Ryan leaned close, and before I could gauge his reaction to the pixie short hair, his fingers were brushing through the choppy dark strands. His eyes searched over it, tugging me closer as his touch tickled around and raked through the nape of my neck.

"It's adorable," he huffed and cupped my face in both hands, "in a you were dying kind of way."

"Ryan!" I scoffed, but a smile spread on my lips. "You think so?"

"I don't know why you hide it?" He said plainly and let me go.

"Because after it was gone, it was hard to look in the mirror and find the girl I was. It was like she had died, and whoever had come home from the hospital was some chemo-monster. If I couldn't look at myself and the kids at school had spread the narrative of a teenage pregnancy. I didn't want more eyes on me. I couldn't handle it."

"Was it scary?" He asked me, his body so still I could barely tell he was breathing.

"At times," I said, "you never know what to expect when the doctors visit."

"Promise me something?" He asked, bringing my hand up to his lips and kissing my knuckles gently.

"What?" I asked, doing my best to ignore the warmth that flooded me.

"I can't change the past. I can't go back and be there for you, but promise me that you'll tell me if you feel sick or scared. You'll let me help?" he asked, his eyes painfully green.

"Nothing bad is going to happen, Ryan," I said to him, scooting closer on the step.

"Convincing me of that will be harder than you think," he said. "Just promise me you'll talk to me. You won't do it alone this time?"

He was serious. Extremely serious.

"Alright," I said, just to quell the intense feelings stirring around behind his eyes.

"And stop wearing these stupid wigs around me. I want to feel your real hair when I touch you, " he whispered, and it made my chest warm.

"On one condition." My lips pressed into a thin, serious line. He wasn't getting everything he wanted that easily. He had to work for something.

Ryan scoffed, "What?"

"You finish your papers *and* you let me help you apply to colleges," I said.

"I'm not getting into college, Rae, not the old-fashioned way." Ryan shook his head in disbelief.

"How about you worry about me, and I'll worry about you?" I said, leaning in closer and pressing my head against his. "Deal?"

He grumbled something under his breath but nodded against my forehead. "Deal."

Ryan didn't seem like the type to drop an issue so intense and move on. From the look in his eyes, I could tell it wouldn't be as simple as telling him the truth and promising to follow through on our deal.

He was going to go through the stages.

Everyone did.

First, he would treat me like I was more fragile than the birthday present he had purchased for me. Then he would research, call people, and read books he never would have thought to open. All to find a solution. Then the denial would come, the idea that cancer doesn't exist if we don't let it. That it's simply a mind game.

The last stage before acceptance would be anger.

He would get pissed off. He would ask me a million questions. Wonder why I'm not more upset about the unfairness of it all. It was only natural for him to go through all of that my parents had, I had, and random people at the hospital had when they saw a sixteen-year-old girl sitting in the radiation chair.

It was inevitable.

"Let's start with the immediate problem: you have a game you need to play in. And you've got very little time left to make that happen because you've been distracted."

"Usually, I would argue with you, but today I'm happy to let you win because there's only two things I need in this world, your love and to win that game." Ryan huffed gently with our foreheads still pressed together, his breath warm on my cheeks.

"That was cheesy," I laughed and scrunched my nose up.

"My backpack is in your bushes around the back," he said with a chuckle before kissing my forehead and pushing off the steps to retrieve it.

I watched him walk away with a thousand thoughts swirling in his mind, his fingers tapping against his thigh as his eyes searched the sky for answers. The stars wouldn't help him, though. They never helped me.

FIELD

Sitting at the island going over his work had taken hours, and before I knew it, the lock on the front door had popped, and my heart dropped into my stomach.

"Don't say a word," I warned Ryan as his eyes drifted over my head to the front door.

I hadn't put my wig back on as per his request, and for some reason, the idea of my parents seeing me like this—messy hair, dirty sweater, half-eaten cake on the island strewn about with a bunch of half-finished English papers—shook my confidence.

Ryan being here would cause my mother to riot, but in the most constricted, fake way her nature would allow. She'd likely thank him for coming to our home before shooing him out the door to scold me for two hours about the rules and regulations of our house and the importance of screening everyone who enters our front door.

"Lorraine?" Her voice echoed through the empty house to the kitchen, and my entire body tensed at the sound.

"In here, Mom," I said.

As she and Dad came around the corner, tired from travel but still looking pristine, Dad stripped from his suit jacket and rolled his sleeves when he stopped in the doorway of the kitchen behind my mother in her pearl dress shirt and matching skirt.

Ryan rose off the stool behind me and straightened out against my back. His breathing was slow and methodical as my father studied him and then looked back at me.

"Who's this?" He asked me as he stepped into the kitchen.

I opened my mouth to explain, but Ryan was faster, and I mumbled a few tame curse words at the sound of his voice. I kept forgetting that his listening skills left much to be desired.

"Ryan Cody, Mayor Field." Ryan stepped out from behind me and held out his hand.

"Robert Cody's boy, you live off Lorne Way, the farm."

"That's correct, sir," Ryan said.

I had to stifle the laughter that uncharacteristically bubbled from me at the sight of Ryan being so polite.

"Your brother, Robert Jr., comes to town hall meetings with him. I've never seen you there." My Dad pointed out. Faces, that was his entire election campaign, and he never forgot a face, which meant he was taking care of everyone in the town. The idea that he could remember *everyone* was absurd, but the town had believed every word and he had been elected and re-elected.

I could feel my mother's gaze on my face as I watched them talk.

It burned like hot metal; unfortunately, I had to sit and take it from her.

"Until I graduate, my focus is on school and baseball, sir."

My Dad's expression tightened at his answer.

"And why are you in my home with my daughter, Mr. Cody?" He asked Ryan.

"She's tutoring me in English, sir," Ryan answered without hesitation.

"Seems your focus slipped." The backhanded comment landed because I watched Ryan's shoulder blades come together beneath his shirt.

"English was never my strong suit, sir, but I reached out for help, and my grade is coming up." I wasn't sure how honest of a statement it was because he hadn't handed in any of his missing assignments yet, and his grade was stagnant, just like his baseball career.

Suspended in time until he figured out how to balance it all in the small pocket of his baseball mitt.

"I hope the time spent with my daughter has helped, but I do ask that if you're coming over to our home, you pick a day when we're home. I'm not comfortable with the idea of you being alone with Lorraine, " he said.

I held in the sigh, grinding my teeth together to keep the frustrated sound deep within me as my mother watched my every move.

"Unfortunately, I wasn't comfortable with her being alone, especially not on her birthday, so I apologize for breaking the rules, but I *will* do it again."

All of the air was sucked from the room in a violent woosh as the words left Ryan's lips. My father's hands curled around the island's edges as he straightened out and hovered over Ryan ominously. My Mother's face was priceless, shock laced with disgust at Ryan's *outburst*.

That's what she would call it. I could hear her voice now, yelling over the sound of my father slamming things in his office after Ryan left.

"It was nice to meet you, Mr. Cody, but it's time you left."

"Yeah, figured as much." He nodded tightly, a few strands of dirty blonde hair falling against his cheeks as he winked at me. "I'll see you at school on Monday." He said, stepping back and reaching around me to grab his bag from the stool behind me. His lips brushing against my cheek was enough to turn them pink as he backed away. "Happy Birthday, Starlight."

I watched as he held his hand to my mother, "Ma'am."

She looked down at it and then over at me with a scowl before curling her arms across her chest.

"Alright," Ryan nodded, his voice low and tight. "Monday," he repeated, and he sidestepped around my mother toward the front door.

The three of us stood in silence as it opened and closed with a loud click.

"How dare you," my Mother sighed. "You know the rules, Lorraine."

"I'm tutoring him. It's for school." I defended quietly, curling in on myself to become smaller as my father rounded the island to hover in front of me.

"Do all of the students you tutor show such affection?" He asked me.

"He's just like that, it was nothing. He was causing a scene because you made him uncomfortable." I argued. "Which you didn't have to do. We weren't doing anything besides homework."

"This is my house, Lorraine, and you are *my* daughter. Start acting like it." Were his next words before leaving the kitchen and me all alone with my mother.

My scolding wasn't through. The second wave was imminent.

"You can't speak to him like that, Lorraine. He's your father, and he's right. You're not allowed to have boys in the house, especially when we're not home."

"I'm not allowed to have *anyone* in the house, and you're *never* home!" I raised my voice as I heard the soft sound of the office door closing.

"You knew what obligations your father had this weekend," she said as if it was okay that they missed my birthday for the tenth time in how many years? It was just like her to make this about them like I was an inconvenience to their personal lives and careers.

She wandered around the kitchen and pulled a bottle of wine from the cabinet, popping it open in my face like we weren't in the middle of an argument.

"It's been like this since I got sick. You both leave me alone as if you can't stand to be around me. You can't catch cancer, mom, it's not viral." I huffed gently, the frustration rising.

"Lorraine," she hissed, "you know that has nothing to do with it. Your father is important to this county and to the state. We have obligations to the state and to the governor."

Yeah, and his big fancy lake house is sixteen hours away.

"I know," I said instead.

"Then why are you acting like this?" She asked, not wanting a lick of the truth but just wanting an answer that would make her feel better about herself as she downed a glass of wine.

"I'm not acting like anything. Ryan was here to get tutored in English; nothing is going on, and you and Dad are acting like he got me pregnant!" I rolled my eyes, and she slammed the glass to the counter.

What about your father's reputation?

"What about your father's reputation?" She said right on cue.

"They barely even know I exist. Tutoring someone from school isn't going to reflect badly on Dad!" I argued, careful to watch my tone with her.

"It's not about the tutoring!" She snapped.

"Oh…" I laughed, the sound hollow and frustrated. Like a long sigh. "This is about who he is, his last name."

"You're the mayor's daughter, Lorraine." My mother said.

"You say that like he's the king. He's the mayor of some backwater Texas shit hole!" I snapped the anger from her judgments bubbling to the surface alongside the need to defend Ryan with every ounce of energy I had.

"Lorraine Field!" She snapped. "Watch your language."

"I'm sorry," I said without meaning a word of it.

"There will be no more tutoring, that boy will no longer be allowed in the house, and I don't even want to see him on the driveway. Do you understand me?" She lowered her tone as her jaw tightened.

"He needs my help!" I argued.

"He's turning you into someone I don't recognize!" My mother snapped, a few pieces of her perfect blonde hair falling from its bun.

"Of course, you don't recognize me. I'm standing up for myself."

"Excuse me?" She shook her head. "Go to your room!"

"Yeah, I'm going," I said, grabbing my little glass figurine and my schoolwork in my arms.

"Don't come down until you're ready to apologize!" She added as I got to the kitchen door.

I turned to look at her and found her looking smaller than usual. Like during the argument she had lost all her bite and didn't seem so scary in my eyes anymore. I smiled, knowing it would piss her off, but I felt free.

"It's not like you would notice if I did, Mom." I shrugged and disappeared upstairs before she could get in another word.

CODY

I knew that knocking on the front door was a bad idea, but I couldn't help myself. She hadn't been at school again on Monday, and on the drive over, I had debated with myself about the possibility that her parents had locked her in the tower of their palace.

I was worried about her, and I was going to be polite and tell her parents to their faces that I was. So I knocked again when no one answered.

After I had left on Saturday, my brain never stopped. I had gone straight to the public library to look through any medical books I could get my hands on, but there wasn't much about leukemia in any of them. There was, however, a ton of medical jargon that I didn't understand and, frankly, only scared the shit out of me and my limited IQ.

When she told me, the first thing I wanted to do was cry.

But I wasn't going to do that in front of her, so I'd waited until their front door shut and cried all the way to the highway. There were far more painful moments in life than my father kicking the shit out of me over skipping school. I just hadn't been aware that I would be subject to such agony so soon after meeting the one person in my life that didn't make me feel like a disaster all the time.

I couldn't believe that whatever God existed could inflict such harm on someone as sweet and smart as Lorraine. My heart throbbed in my chest as if someone had shoved a hundred tiny shards of glass into it. It was dramatic, and for about three steps off her porch, it had felt like the world was ending.

But she was in remission. She was healthy, *for now*, and that's what mattered. But why couldn't I stop dwelling on every little detail, all the small things that could contribute to her getting sick again? Did it even work that way, or was I spinning up issues to make the possibility more tangible?

I just wanted to spend the rest of my life with her.

Stupid, foolish thoughts of a seventeen-year-old in love.

I didn't even know if she wanted the same or if I could give her the life she wanted, but I knew that I would try. I would be whatever she wanted or needed me to be, as long as she allowed me to love her, healthy or sick, every day.

So I sat up in my room and finished what bits of my papers I could do without her help and I cried some more, so hard that by the time I was finished, I'd given myself the worst headache I've ever had. So I crawled into the bed and vowed to myself as I pressed my face into the shabby pillow that I would protect her from everything until the end of my days.

And then I woke up, went to school, and searched for her in the halls and the library only to panic when she wasn't there *again*. I skipped the last period to make sure she was okay, but now after two knocks no one was answering the door, and my mind was spinning out of control again.

Maybe they took her out of town, swept her away, and I wouldn't see her for months again? I slammed my head on the door again, and this time, it swung open to Mrs. Field in a dark blazer and a nasty look on her face. Somewhere underneath the scowl line and the exhausted plastic surgery, she sort of looked like Lorraine. They shared the same vast blue eyes, but Mrs. Field's were darkened by her disdain for life and my presence.

"Ma'am, is Lorraine home?" I asked politely.

"No, she's at school. Where you should be, " she said and started to close the door in my face, but I put my hand up to stop her.

"See, there's the thing, she's not at school. I searched everywhere for her, and you and I both know that Rae would never skip," I said, my fingers pressing into the expensive wood as Mrs. Field's eyes raked over them angrily.

"It's none of your business where my daughter is, Mr. Cody. I see she didn't inform you that you weren't allowed back on our property," She sneered, the harsh lines around her mouth deepening.

"She couldn't, because she wasn't at school and I probably wouldn't have listened even if she had," I said honestly, "you see I have this condition called persistent shithead, my Mom screams that fact at me regularly, so you're going to have to do a lot better than '*you're not allowed on our property*' to keep me from Rae."

"Her name is Lorraine." She corrected me with a snarl. "And if you don't leave my porch Mr. Cody, I'll call the cops, and your mother can scream it at the sheriff in town."

"Tomato, tomatoe." I shrugged. "Usually, I'd fight you on it and my mom yells at *my Uncle* at least three times a week. Combined with how politely you asked me, I'll go. But can you tell Rae I came to see her? Just because you hate me doesn't mean she does and I don't want her to think I abandoned her."

Mrs. Field's eyes narrowed on me at the last confession, her features softening just for a moment before returning to the usual hardened expression as she shut the door in my face.

"That was easy," I said with a chuckle and walked toward the edge of the porch. I walked down the driveway over to Landry's, popped the latch on the fence, and wandered into the backyard. There were three loose boards connecting their yards, and with Mrs. Field thinking that she had won our little interaction, I was free to slip into their yard, and she'd be none the wiser.

"Cody?" Landry was chucking balls at the back wall of his two-story house and cocked his eyebrow at me. "Why aren't you at school?"

"Why aren't you?" I asked him back.

"Touche," he sighed and chucked the ball again. Are you going to see Lon—" he stopped himself and looked over his shoulder at me. "Lorraine?"

"Yes, I've been banished from their step."

"That's never stopped you before," Landry said.

"Exactly." I kicked the board loose, and he laughed.

"Hey, there's a party at the beach for Coop. You should get her out of her room." Landry suggested unexpectedly, and it caused me to pause halfway through the small break in the fence.

"Why?" I asked, cautious about his sudden change in tone.

"Listen, man, just because I don't understand it doesn't mean I don't see it. You like her. You have since you wandered into my house asking about her. I've lived next to them my entire life and have never spoken more than a sentence to

Lorraine. She deserves some fun, and I mean, I guess she's kinda pretty when she's not squirreled away up there with her nose in a book."

"I'm going to forget you said the last part." I smiled at him, "But thanks, man."

He turned his back to me and left me to my business as the rhythmic thump of the baseball hitting the back of the house returned. I crept along the yard, keeping to the tree line close to the side of the house, scooping a handful of white rocks from their perfect garden bed. It took me a few seconds to pause and watch the kitchen window, but I managed to get to Lorraine's window without being noticed.

I chucked one rock at a time to the window pane above me, knowing full well that she was in her room. There was not a single other place she would be. She didn't answer after the first rock, so I threw another and waited.

"Come on, Rae," I swore under my breath and chucked another.

As I arched my arm back to throw another, the window latch clicked, and the pane slid up with the shove of two perfect hands.

"There you are," I whispered up at her, "took you long enough."

"What are you doing?" Lorraine hissed. She was wearing one of her wigs, and now that I knew what they were, they bothered me more than before.

"Counting the hours I spent loving you," I smiled when she scowled at my cheesy behavior. I loved how her nose scrunched up and her soft lips were pursed together. "I've come to break you out of your tower."

"You know, when I imagined this moment, I expected a lot more Shakespere..." her brows scrunched together.

"I could sing you the lyrics to *Change the World*? But after we revisit that part about imagining this..." I teased her, and she just shook her head.

"I can't sneak out, Ryan," she said quietly.

"You can't, or you won't?" I asked her, and her fingers flexed around the window, giving away her answer. "Rae...we both know they won't even notice." I didn't want to be mean about it. Being a trophy on a shelf in her own home had to be exhausting. It wasn't a joke or a punchline. It was heartbreaking.

"I'll get in so much trouble..." Lorraine sighed.

"You're already locked in your room. What's the worst that could happen?" I asked her.

She thought about it for a moment, *really thought about it*. Her lips pressed into a thin line, and she looked around at her room behind her.

"Rae, look at me," I said to her. When our eyes connected, the world slowed down around us, the birds grew quiet, and the clouds stopped spinning. At that moment I figured out that it was possible for love to move heaven and earth because every time she looked at me with those ocean eyes, it did. Heaven spun in different directions, and the world stopped to watch her with me. "They don't *deserve* your obedience, so get dressed and climb down here because we have things to do."

"Climb down?" She panicked instantly and looked at the distance between us. "Absolutely not!"

"Well, you can't walk out the front door…" I laughed at her.

"Yes, I can," she said with a huff, pulling back from the window and gently shutting it. The next ten minutes of waiting for her felt like an eternity, and I almost chucked the few rocks I had left up at the window to check in on her.

"Stop it," she chuffed as she rounded the corner of her house into the confined space between the siding and the fence.

"I was getting worried," I tossed the rocks aside.

"What was so important that you just had to plan a prison break?" She asked me as I reached out and felt the long wig between my fingers. I hated that thing. When I didn't answer she wrapped her hand around my wrist and smiled up at me. "Ryan, focus."

"There's a beach party. They're throwing it for Coop's birthday."

"Mark Cooper?" She scoffed.

"…Yes," I laughed at the way she had reacted to it.

"You realize all of those people hate me or pretend I don't exist?" She said as I linked our fingers and quietly led her back around the fence.

"Dinner first, and then the party." I ignored the worry in her voice. "Mary will probably be there. You like her, don't you?" I asked her. I had seen them together occasionally at school. Mary considered them friends, but I wasn't sure Lorraine even knew that.

"I... yeah, I guess so. This is still a bad idea," She said.

"Yeah, but there's no fun in playing it safe, and I won't let anyone say anything to you." I turned on her before we broke out onto the street and dropped to her eye level. I won't let anyone ever make you feel small again. Okay?" I said to her. She paused for a moment before nodding. Still unsure, the trust was slowly bridging the gap between her nervous concern and my reckless abandon.

"Okay."

FIELD

After a quick stop at Duke's for fries and a shake, Ryan took my hand and led me back down through the gates toward the Cooper house. It was one of the only ones that looked out over the small lake that separated our town from the next. Most families had vacation houses; otherwise, the Cooper house would have always been dubbed the party house when their parents left.

Until that night, I had never thought about what Mary did during those. She didn't seem like the type to enjoy her older brother's shenanigans, but what did I know? We had only spoken once or twice before, and I was making the same assumptions that everyone had made about me.

The house was already packed with people, but Ryan bypassed the steps and wandered around the side of the house to a small wooded path that led down through some trees to a private section of sand with a raging fire and only a handful of people from school.

I recognized a few of them. Landry tossed a football in the sand with a few of the other baseball players. His older sister, Margaret, was settled into a chair with her boyfriend and a few of their friends, laughing and drinking loudly.

"Look," Ryan pointed down the beach a bit to where Mary sat, her toes tucked into the sand, staring out over the water with a book in her hand.

The fact that he had noticed the budding friendship left a warm feeling in my chest as he pulled me toward Landry.

"Hey, you made it. I was worried there for a second that Mayor Field locked you in his dungeon," Landry joked and gave Ryan a pat on the back. "I don't think I've ever seen you at a party, Lorraine," he said to me, and I braced for the joke. "It's nice," He said instead and pointed to something behind me. "There's drinks in the cooler. We tried convincing Mary to play, but she flipped me off and wandered the beach. You should see if you can get her to join us," he smiled at me and jogged a few steps back before slinging the ball over his head to his friend.

"You want anything to drink?" Ryan asked, nudging my shoulder, and I shook my head at him.

"I'm going to make a friend," I smiled at him, and his mouth turned upward, mirroring mine.

"That's my girl," he teased and released my hand. "Here," he knelt down in front of me and patted his knee for my foot before untying my laces and slipping them off with the sock. "Other one," he hummed and repeated the process. He gently gripped my calf with an encouraging squeeze before rising and kissing my forehead. "Have fun," he added, kicking off his boots before ducking toward the cooler with my shoes in his hands.

I walked through the warm sand toward Mary, whose attention was on her book. I sunk into the sand next to her. "Hey," I said, and she looked up at me with confusion painted across her cute round face.

"Hi..." she said slowly as she closed her book. "You came to a... party?" She said.

I laughed at her hesitation, "Ryan snuck me out."

"Oh..." she said, looking over my shoulder at the group of players now getting rowdy in the sand close to the water's edge. "*Oh!*" Mary gasped with a tiny laugh. "Are you two like..."

"I don't even know where to start," I said gently.

"From the beginning, duh!" Mary set her book aside and gave me her full attention as I went through what had happened for the last week and a half. Saying it all out loud to another person made me feel crazy, but the more I talked about Ryan, the more I realized that he wasn't the only one with ridiculous feelings.

"You guys are like a movie!" She hummed and fell back into the sand with a long sigh. "He really tells you that he loves you every *single* time?" She asked.

"Every time. At first, I thought he was crazy, but now I kinda..." I trailed off and looked over my shoulder at him. The wind pushed around the fabric of his shirt as he lifted his arm to throw the ball, exposing the soft lines of his tanned stomach and the swooping lines of his pelvis leading into the top of his jeans.

The sun was setting behind him, painting the sky with pinks and purples that framed him in a soft haze, making him look more like a fantasy and less like a teenage boy. He cheered as the ball landed cleanly in the hands of another player. He whipped his baseball hat around his head until the brim was backward. He wrapped Landry into a celebratory bear hug, both laughing and fighting in the early summer air.

"Wait for it?" Mary laughed, "I would too. Ryan Cody is a dreamboat."

The ball soared across the beach and landed at our feet with a splash of sand that made Mary giggle, but I was too lost in my overwhelming need to tell Ryan just how much I *loved* him. *When the hell did that happen?*

Mary stood up and chucked the ball back with surprising speed and accuracy. It landed between Landry's palms, and he gave her a wink. "Thanks, little Coop," he smirked at her and Mary turned about nine different shades of pink before sinking back into the sand with me.

"What the heck was that?" I asked her, and she shrugged.

"He always flirts with me, but I think they're all scared of my brother, so none of them ask me out... It kinda sucks." Mary said quietly, "Landry is the cutest."

"You have a crush on Landry?" I gasped and stared at her.

"Shut up, you can't tell anyone!" Mary poked me as laughter bubbled from her.

"Who am I going to tell? You're my only friend." I said.

"Mm, not true." She nodded to the horizon and caused me to turn.

Ryan and Landry stood shoulder to shoulder, staring at us, a massive smile on his handsome face. The one that curled a little to the left and showed off his perfect, sharp smile.

"That boy is in deep, Lorraine." Another small laugh left Mary's lips. I didn't have a proper response, so I just sat wondering if it was possible to love someone you've only known for a week as if you had been loving them your entire life. And I believed it, looking at him, the way his eyes twinkled under the setting sun.

"Hey, you want a snack? Tyson bought way too much food on Dad's credit card and there's no way we can finish it before they get home next week." Mary rambled and pushed up from the sand with her hand out to me.

"Yeah, sure," I said, taking her hand and getting up from the sand. Ryan stepped forward, his eyes always watching, but I shook my head at him. *I'm fine.* He nodded back, two of his fingers coming up, and patted the space over his heart twice. I'd never seen him do it before but I could feel his reassurance like he was standing directly beside me, it spread through me like a warm safety. A quiet promise between the two of us.

The house was packed; people occupied every piece of furniture, even the ones not meant for sitting or lounging. Tyson Cooper, a male copy of Mary with dark hair and big brown eyes full of wonder and light, was leading what sounded like the most animated game of spin the bottle in the living room with a group of kids who had graduated the year before.

"This way." She led me through the hallway toward a separate room with a closed door, opening it to reveal a pantry stocked with just about every single junk food I'd ever seen and hadn't been allowed to eat in the last two years. "Take your pick," Mary said.

After collecting an armful of candy and chips, we decided that retreating to her room would be more fun for both of us. However, she wanted to grab a couple of cans of soda before we did, so we moved back through the house to the kitchen.

"Shit," Mary swore as we rounded the corner to Cadence and her groupies. "Cadence... looking pretty as always," Mary sneered quietly and moved around them, but my route was blocked; all I could do was stand and stare at the three of them.

"Who the hell invited you here?" Cadence asked and the other two giggled in chorus of what could only be described as snakes hissing.

"Ryan," I said with all the confidence I could muster, which wasn't much when his name came out a stuttered mess. *It's two syllables, Lorraine...*

"R..R...Ryan," Paisley teased, and Georgia lost it laughing, which only made me feel worse about the stumble.

It was hard to find the girls buried beneath the monsters when they cornered and teased me like this. I tried to remember what Mary had said about them, but nothing seemed to stick long enough for me to find my confidence and fight back. They all smelled sickly of cranberry juice and vodka, drunk off their faces and looking for a target.

"Ryan's community service is almost up, loser, and you'll go back to being the loner you were before," Georgia added when she had composed herself.

That made Cadence snort before a wicked smile plastered on her face. "You might be rich, Lorraine, but parties like these…aren't for people like *you*."

I opened my mouth to excuse myself, stepping back into a wall of warmth.

"You're going to have to explain that one to me, Caddy, because I'm not really sure what you're trying to say?" Ryan's voice floated over the four of us as his hand wrapped around my stomach and pulled me tightly to him.

"You know exactly what I mean, Ryan. She's a loser, she barely speaks, and it's almost cruel the way you parade her around like you actually care." Cadence narrowed her eyes on him, but there was a sweetness to her voice that wasn't there before.

A week ago, not knowing Ryan or having been convinced otherwise, her words might have allowed the doubt to seep in through the cracks. But with him wrapped around me, I didn't have a single doubt that he cared. I *knew* he did. I could feel it vibrating from him.

Ryan chuckled, his breath warm on my ear as his fingers dug into my stomach and he leaned forward into me. "What it sounds like is you're acting like a whiny bitch because you want attention, but I have news for you Caddy," he said and she flinched at the nickname. "Not everything is about you, and the *sooner* you learn that the sooner you can start working on your lifelong dream of being a trophy wife to the next wash-out car salesman. Our town would go under without people like you."

Cadence looked like she might be sick as she bristled from his comments and tightened her hot pink claws around her cup. "You've changed, Ryan Cody."

"You say that like you know me, Cadence." He sneered with another small laugh as she started to back away. "One more thing," he said as the three of them started to exit the kitchen, "if you ever look at Lorraine wrong again, if I hear one rumor that even remotely sounds like it came from any of you, we'll have this conversation again, but I won't be nice next time."

Mary snorted, scaring me after forgetting she was also in the kitchen with us.

"Run along now," she said to them as they had already started disappearing. "She's going to spiral about that car salesman comment for a week."

"Good," Ryan pressed his lips to my cheek. "Are you okay?" he asked quietly against my ear, and I nodded. "How about a walk?" he asked me, and I opened my mouth to tell him that I was going to go hang out with Mary, but she shook her head at me and took the bag of chips from my arms.

"I'll see you at school tomorrow," Mary said with a smile and wandered through the house.

"Sorry, I interrupted your...whatever that was..." Ryan said.

"It was nothing," I said, turning out of his arms and wiggling my fingers at him to take. Without pause, he intertwined our hands and led us from the back of the house down to the beach. Everything had quieted down outside, and the bonfire was crackling into the dark sky, which was the only light source next to the moon. "Thank you for standing up for me," I said as he settled next to me in the sand.

"I'd do anything for you, Rae," He responded with conviction, "However, when it comes to them, promise you'll never listen to a word they say. It all comes from jealousy and malice, none of it is true."

I turned to look at him and found his brows tight with worry, his green eyes watching me carefully, almost as if he expected me to doubt him.

"I know," I said to him and squeezed my hand around his tighter. There was not a shred of doubt to be found as we sat under the stars with the heat from the fire licking at our cold skin.

CODY

I picked her up twenty minutes ago and still haven't said a word to her about where we're going or what we're doing. I can feel how nervous she is. She hates surprises almost as much as she hates sneaking out, but we were getting better at it. I'm so glad she found her rebellious side because it was hard to go those few hours after school without her.

She was wearing some adorable loose sweater that hung around her collarbone and showed off her shoulder. If I wasn't driving, I would lean over and press my lips to the bare skin but I'd settle for being distracted because I had her in my truck, and life was good. My last paper was finished, sliding around on the dashboard as I took small corners. I finally found a memory to write about, getting over the fear that it had to be some grand childhood memory that shaped my entire life. I found my voice, picked a memory and just wrote.

It might not be good, but it's finished, which was what mattered.

I had held up my side of the deal. I had finished all my missing assignments.

I could tell she was proud of me. She had read it quietly for the first half of the drive and asked me silly questions about certain moments, only to reward me with a small kiss at the only red light in town.

"Where are we going?" Lorraine asked as I finally pulled the truck off the highway toward one of the massive corn fields surrounding our town.

"You're insanely impatient for a girl that only just started leaving her room on a regular basis," I laughed and slowed the truck down to line up with the other cars.

I watched as she shifted in the seat, tucking her feet beneath her butt to raise up through the open window, her hair blowing around in the light breeze as her eyes twinkled.

"Is this the drive-in?" She asked me, sliding back down into her seat and I nodded at her as she closed the gap between us on the bench. "I've never been!" She squealed and kissed a peppered line of tiny kisses along my cheek to the corner of my mouth.

It was nearly impossible not to get distracted after that. The heat rose in my neck, and all I wanted to do was park the truck and kiss her back. But the line moved, and I put my hand out to push her gently back against the seat before I started to move again. The line moved at a creeping pace as people paid for their tickets.

Her body was pressed against the dashboard to peer out the front window at the giant screen. She wiggled the entire time we were in line and only settled down when I found a parking spot. "How are we supposed to watch a movie like this?" She asked when I backed the truck into the spot.

"Your excitement is clouding your sense," I laughed and cut the engine. I hopped from the cab, moved to open her door, and helped her out. I led her around the back and popped the tailgate to show her the second part of my surprise. Blankets and a few pillows lined the bed.

She looked over at me with the stars in her eyes and smiled sweetly.

"Help me?" She asked, and without thought, I lifted her to the tailgate so she could get comfy, but not before wrapping my arms around her and tugging her impossibly close for a kiss. Her lips met mine with a slow and sweet smile. Rows of cars piled in around us, filling the parking lot with chatter and laughter until the movie started.

"The Outsiders?" Lorraine gasped as the movie started. "How did you know?"

"Your school-lent copy of it has seen better days, almost like you've read it a hundred times," I said, proud of myself.

"I have," she huffed and turned to me. "Thank you," she said, "this is really nice."

"Anything for you, Starlight," I said without skipping a beat. "I'll go grab us some snacks, stay here…" I reached around her and wrapped her in the blanket, tucking it into her hands to keep her warm.

The walk to the concession booth was quick, but the line was long. I spotted Landry standing a few people back from the window and skipped into the line with him, throwing my arm over his shoulder.

"Hey man," he said, leaning into me with a smile. "You bring Lorraine out?"

I nodded, "I just came to grab her some popcorn. What are you doing here? You hate Patrick Swayze…" I looked him up and down.

"But little Cooper doesn't," Landry wiggled his eyebrows at me. "And what she wants, she gets."

"I never thought I would see the day that a girl conquered Landry Matthews, let alone one as spacey and weird as Mary Cooper." I laughed.

"I guess once you slow down and really take in your surroundings, you find things that have always been there," Landry said in a tone I had never heard from him. It was quiet and genuine. I stared at him for a moment before pressing the back of my hand to his head.

"You sure you aren't sick, buddy?" I teased as he pushed my hand away.

"I'm starting to think Coop has been keeping us away from his little sister for a good reason. She's *funny*, man, and honest…but in a way I can't explain. She says shit, and it's like it's the funniest thing I've ever heard. Even when it's at my expense."

"Sounds like you're in love," I told him as we approached the counter.

"Give me a week, and I'll let you know when the fog clears," Landry smiled and turned to the overly annoyed girl behind the counter. He ordered two of everything and paid. "My treat. Don't tell Lorraine we're here until the back half of the movie?" he asked me.

My brows furrowed in confusion.

"At least let me get in a makeout before this turns into a double date. Once Mary finds out she's here, the conversation will never end." Landry laughed and his usual irritation toward a girl isn't there. It's just a playful adoration.

"Alright," I laughed and took my popcorn and the bottles of pop from him, awkwardly shoving them in my arms for the walk back to Lorraine. She was right where I left her, eyes wide, staring up at the big screen. The soft dialogue between *Soda-pop* and *Darry* floated through the open slide window of the cab. She looked so happy it clenched tightly in my chest. The sweet swoop of her nose and the delicate way her lips moved as she caught on to the writing that she recognized from the book. She was beloved and she had no clue.

"If I could spend the rest of my life watching you watch things you loved, I'd die a happy man, Rae," I whispered to her over the hushed sounds of the movie as I climbed up into the bed. I handed her the popcorn and settled down behind her with my back against the cab before wrapping her up and pulling her against my chest.

She grumbled a little, her eyes' attention on the movie faltering as I got comfortable, but she relaxed against my chest, her fingers digging through the popcorn to find the buttered pieces.

"You know, Dally only ever wanted Johnny to succeed. He might have been a little rough and backward but they were family." She said quietly with a few tears as Ponyboy read over Johnny's last letter. "And he might have never seen one, but now he lives in the sunsets with Johnny. They'll always be able to find them there. Robert Frost was wrong," she said.

"About what?" I asked her and kissed her shoulder.

"He said *'nothing gold can stay.'* But he's wrong, gold can stay if we try hard enough to remember them being gold, they'll stay that way forever," Her voice was choked up when she finished and I knew she was crying but instead of trying to make it better I just let her have the moment.

I couldn't bear to tell her it was just a book; her words were so soft and she extended such a caring understanding to these fictional characters as if she was a part of their family. After reading a book so many times, I guess she believed she was heart and soul. A world where she was free... it would have made her laugh and cry like she had during the entire movie.

"One day, like Dally, you'll become the stars," I said to her, pressing a kiss to the top of her head as the credits started to roll. "Not everyone will know you're there or appreciate it but that's where you belong. With the stars."

Her body tensed in mine, but her fingers wrapped around my forearm as she tucked her face against my chest.

"Don't cry more, Rae," I said to her with a laugh.

"You can't say the most profound, idiotic thing and expect me to keep my cool after watching Johnny die!" She practically wailed. I rested my hand on her hand, fingers curling into her hair as she tried to calm down.

"I love you," I whispered against the top of her head.

"Even when I'm crying?" She grumbled.

"Especially." I laughed.

It wasn't much longer before the screen went black, and I was helping her down from the truck bed and driving her home. I parked down the street and walked with her up to the house, standing just out of view of her front windows with my hand tangled into hers.

"They're never going to accept that I'm some poor farmer kid," I said quietly, my confidence shaking under the ominous mansion. Everything about it mocked my inability to provide her with that down the road. Our future would never look so rich.

"Since when do you care what they think?" She asked me as her fingers brushed my jaw and forced me to look at her.

"I only care about you," I said. "I want out of this town, Rae, and I want to take you with me, but..." I scowled and took a moment to collect all of my scattered thoughts. "I'll never be able to give you that," I nodded to her perfect white fence and rose bushes.

"Good," she laughed, the sound unexpected. "I don't want to live or die in a house like that, cold and unwelcoming. Empty hallways and untouched furniture."

"You don't mean that you're just trying to make me feel better," I said, and she shook her head.

"Until you came along, there wasn't a single person who had ever noticed me. Not the way you do..." she smiled up at me. "You took me to the drive-in tonight based on the sole fact that you've *seen* how well I read my copy of the book. That's more than just throwing money at me and *making me comfortable*." Lorraine said the last part with venom. "I want to live," she said, "I want to laugh and love...I want to struggle and learn." She added. "I want that with you.

I don't care where we go or where we live. As long as I have you and the stars, I'll be happy."

I stared at her, every word she said with confidence and a startling lack of hesitation.

"And I hate roses," she said with a scoff, "lavender bushes, I want a thousand lavender bushes."

"Alright, alright," I threw my hands up in surrender. "Love *and* lavender bushes," I said.

CODY

An A.

"Congratulations, Mr. Cody. Looks like you'll get to play in your game."

I stared down at the paper in my shaky hands and tried not to scream in the middle of English class when I saw that ugly red marker in the shape of an A.

I got a fucking A!

When the bell rang, I collected my bag and beelined for the library. The door slammed against the wall, and the librarian startled up from her desk with a scowl on her face. I apologized in passing and crept through the main space before checking all the aisles, but Lorraine was nowhere to be found.

"Again?" I swore and jogged down to my truck. I didn't care what her parents said. I wanted to show her my paper and my grade. I only wanted to celebrate with her. The drive up to the gated community was longer than any other day I've driven it, but when I finally found myself on her street, my heart was ready to pound out of my chest.

I don't know why I was so nervous. It was as if she would tell me our friendship was over now that I didn't need her help anymore or anything, but I couldn't breathe as I knocked on the door.

It took a moment, but before I could knock again, footsteps approached the door, and it unlocked. Lorraine's father stood with tired eyes in what appeared to be an old suit with a loose tie.

"Mr. Cody?" He narrowed his gaze on me, rolling from head to toe as he sighed. "She's not home, and you shouldn't be here."

"Where is she then?" I asked him, ignoring the judgmental tone to his dry voice.

"She's out with her Mother," he answered quickly and aimed to close the door in my face, but I stopped him. The Field family had a habit of that closing doors on people in the middle of conversations.

"Out where?" I asked. His answer created a tidal wave of unsettling worry.

"Son, it's none of your business," he answered, and that time, he managed to get the door closed. I groaned and flexed my hands at my sides, tempted to bang on the door again.

I looked around the porch to find traces of her without luck. None of her usual were lying around, no sweaters or blankets. Even the space where her telescope occupied was empty, leaving three small, worn-in circles where the tripod typically stood.

My heart hadn't slowed, and my throat felt sticky as I snuck around the side of the house to chuck a few rocks at her bedroom window, just hoping that the nauseating gut feeling I had was wrong.

I threw rock after rock, the last one hitting so hard it created a tiny splinter of glass. I stepped back against the fence with a sad huff. *There's a chance she is just out with her mom...* I thought, but that worry still licked at the back of my mind, and I couldn't leave it be.

Spinning on my heel, I followed the fence and shoved my way into Landry's backyard, hoisting my weight onto the barbecue and then onto his balcony. I clicked the lock on his sliding door and dipped inside of his empty room.

"Landry?" I called out without an answer. I kicked around his room, trying to figure out where he had gone before exiting his room, wandering downstairs, and calling out to him again.

"He's not home," Landry's older sister, Margaret, stood in the kitchen eating a bowl of cereal with a magazine spread open on the island. Her long red hair was braided back over her shoulders, and her attention was minimal as I moved closer. "How did you even get in here?"

"His door doesn't lock properly on his balcony... where is he?" I asked, setting my bag down.

"Out with that Cooper girl," She said, pushing around her frosted flakes.

"Mary," I corrected her, and she shrugged her shoulders. "Hey, have you seen Lorraine?" I asked her. It was a long shot that she knew anything. On the best of days, Margaret was there for a total of an hour when she wasn't self-involved or staring at herself in a mirror. Half the guys on the team only hung out here because she frequently paraded around in her bathing suit, but I never found the appeal of her.

To me, she looked like Landry was wearing a wig.

I flinched when Margaret looked up from the magazine, "Landry didn't tell you?" She asked me, and I shook my head. "Last night, the ambulance was here. Mrs. Field and her daughter both left on it. I think the girl is sick again. She was strapped down to the thingy..."

"The gurney?" I asked, the words sticky in my dry throat as my head began to spin. It was back. She was sick again.

"Yeah, that thing." She snapped her fingers and went back to her magazine without a second thought about the worry on my face.

Panic flooded my body, and my fingers went numb as I collected my bag from the floor and slung it back over my shoulders. "Do you know what hospital they took them to?" I asked before leaving on the off chance that she had more information.

Perhaps something that didn't make me want to crumble into a ball on their kitchen floor. But my knees were shaky, and my breath was shallow as I waited for her to process the question.

"I heard Dad say that they were taking her to some fancy hospital in the city, that whatever it was, it was bad." Margaret's eyes stayed glued on the pages, and it made me want to scream, but it wasn't her fault, and it wouldn't do anything...it wouldn't make me feel better no matter how badly I wanted to expel the emotions from my chest.

"Alright, thanks..." I said before leaving the house and starting back over to the Field house. I banged on the door again, harder this time, and it wasn't long before Mr. Field had the door open. His expression was annoyance mixed with anger as he registered that I had returned.

"Where did they take her? What hospital?" I demanded an answer, not willing to be pushed around again.

"Go home, Mr. Cody." He said, stepping over the threshold with his shoulders pinned back. "My daughter is no concern to you."

"What don't you people get?" I snapped, it happened. I knew that it was the death of my chances to ever see Lorraine again in a way that didn't involve us sneaking around and hiding but God, it felt good. "I will show up here, kicking and screaming, every single day until you tell me where she is, Mayor Field. I don't care if you call the cops. I don't care if you pull strings that ruin my life. I will be here for *her*."

"If she's sick again, you have to tell me because I'll go insane not knowing. I know that I'm not rich or smart. The standards you have set for Rae are mountains I could never climb! I'm fully aware that *she's too good for me.*" I was seething in his silence. "The thing is, sir, we don't get to decide for her. Tell me where she is so I can go see her, and if she doesn't want me there, she can send me away. I just *want* to help her through all this, and you keep blocking me from getting to her."

He watched me throw my fit, letting me get everything off my chest with a straight face before he stepped back into the house, his hand ready to shut the door.

"What you want isn't important," he said before closing the door in my face.

"Hey," the ball hit me in the shoulder inside of me, soaring into my mitt from across the field. Landry's voice a hair too late to warn me about the incoming wave of pain. "Where the hell are you today?" He asked, jogging over to me.

"Have you heard anything about Rae?" I asked him when he stopped in front of me. I rubbed out the pain in my shoulder. It would bruise good but the stinging sensation was already starting to fade. Which was more than I could say about the agony in my chest that I had been carrying around for three days. *Three fucking days.*

I'd show up on their steps every day after school, but after Monday, they stopped answering the door. I didn't even know if Lorraine was home or still in the hospital. But I knew she was okay. I could feel it in my bones.

On the third day, Mayor Field called the sheriff's office, and my Uncle Cael waited for me at the gate as I exited the community.

"What the hell do you think you're doing harassing the mayor?" He asked with his arms crossed over his chest. *"He can press charges, Ryan. Cut it out."*

"They won't tell me what's going on! Their daughter, Lorraine, she's my girlfriend and she's missing. Maybe I should file a police report!" I snapped.

His expression hardened. *"Take your truck home, do your homework, and stop harassing the Mayor,"* he ordered. *"I mean it, Ryan."*

I hadn't been back in twelve hours, but I was tempted to see how far my uncle would go. Was it worth fighting my Dad over tossing me in a cell?

"No, Dad and Mom were talking about it yesterday. It sounded bad..." Landry trailed off. "Little Cooper is going to try to go over to see her. I told her if she has any news, you're the first person she tells."

"Thanks, man, and thank Mary," I said with a curt nod, my eyes filling with water.

"Listen, Ryan... I didn't know Rae was sick like that, and I'm sorry for giving her a hard time," he said sincerely.

"No one knew. We shouldn't have been treating her that way anyway," I snapped, not at him, just because I couldn't stop the frustration from bubbling up. "I'm sorry, I'm just—"

"Worried," Landry finished for me. "You're allowed to be, man. We all see how you look at her. We know what's at stake, but you also have a place to be... a game to win. That's gotta matter."

"I know, I know!" I said, wetting my bottom lip and tilting my chin to the sky to stop the tears that threatened to fall. "I'm trying, alright."

"Our futures ride on this game, Cody. You're future, and if you want a chance at giving Rae the one she deserves, you have to win this with us. We need you." He clapped his hand to my shoulder and leveled with me.

"Okay, alright!" I shoved him back and rolled out my shoulders.

After the longest practice of our lives, I ended up on the floor of Landry's bedroom watching *Tremors* while Mary and him made out on his bed. I tilted my head backward and could see Lorraine's window at a skewed angle, which only made me more sad.

"Do you think she's okay?" I asked, my voice breaking through the volume of the TV and the soft sounds of them giggling at each other from the bed.

"What?" Mary was the first to respond, her head peeking out over the mattress to look at me.

"Do you think Rae is okay?" I pushed up onto my elbows and put my attention on Mary.

"I don't think Mr. Field would be home if she wasn't," she said, but her eyes told a different story—they were so sad and soft. She was just as worried as I was.

"Maybe you're right, I hope you are, but..." I trailed off, letting the darker thoughts invade the light spaces that Mary was trying to create for me.

"I'll go over tomorrow. Mr. Field will be more receptive to me, and I'll try to figure out what's going on. You have a game to win."

She was right, but deep down, the game was starting to matter less and less.

CODY

"Alright, boys, bring it in," Coach said, holding out his arms to us. We all formed a loose huddle in the dugout. The lights above the diamond burned bright and buzzed in tandem with the overwhelming noise from the crowd.

It was hard enough to think, let alone listen to whatever bullshit speech Coach was about to dole out. Today's game against Perrin wouldn't be an easy win, less so because we were the away team. The chant coming from the bleachers was solely for the Perrin Pumas, with very little support flooding in from town for us.

Parents and a few friends had made the three-hour trip to the town over, but not enough to drown out the constant reminder that we were in enemy territory. Every mile we drove out of town tore a small strip off my already hemorrhaging heart. I missed Lorraine. I missed her more than any seventeen-year-old boy should miss anyone. But I couldn't stop the feelings once they had started. I didn't have control over the monster that formed inside of me.

Life didn't have the same glow without her around.

"Cody, pay attention!" Coach snapped, and his hand clapped against the back of my head. "We go out hard, we keep our swings loose and our throws tight. No funny business today. There's too much riding on this game, not only for the school but for the few of you phasing out next year. The scouts are here. Make them pay attention."

"Yes, Coach!" We all barked in unison.

"On the count of three," he said and counted us into a tight cheer that did nothing for our nerves.

Perrin was tough; they played dirty, and all their guys looked like they were thirty years old. After missing nearly two weeks of games... I felt out of practice. All my muscles were tighter than usual, my throat was dry, and my fingers were stiff as I grabbed my bat from the fenced-out area.

I dug my heel into the sand to ground myself and closed my eyes, but Lorraine was there, in the darkness, with her serene smile and glassy blue eyes. *One day, my kids would have those eyes, her smile, her heart,* I thought. *One day, I would be enough for her.*

"You alright?" Landry's voice cut through the peace like a hot knife, and I opened my eyes. The rush of an inordinate amount of noise flowed back in around me, and my bubble popped.

"Yeah, I'll be fine," I said, but his fingers curled around my shoulder. "I'm a mess, but I've played in worse conditions," I admitted under his gaze.

Landry watched me for a second longer before backing away to his position on deck. In any other game, on any other day, I would have fought for first at-bat, but today, I was *scared*. The Perrin pitcher knew it too because as I stepped into the batter's back, a sick smile spread across his ugly face, and he turned to give his first baseman a look that meant trouble.

I did my best to fill my lungs with fresh air, to focus on the smell of damp grass, and turned over sand. I counted carefully to ten in my head before stepping in on the Ump's call and tightening my hands on the bat.

The pitcher stepped back, his body angled toward me with his hand in his glove and his eyes baring down on my shoulders. I watched him count in his head before pulling his arm back and releasing the ball. It hurled toward me, and before I could register what was going on, the ball was in the catcher's glove, and I was on strike one.

"Come on, Cody. Focus." Coach grumbled from the dugout, just loud enough for me to heal. For a man who shrugged off me missing today's game, he sure was putting a lot on my shoulders. The stress was enough to make my back leg shake as the pitcher aimed to embarrass me a second time.

I inhaled again, steadying myself for the incoming pitch. I swung hard this time but still managed to fuck it up. The ball jumped far right and was called foul the second it left the box. I stepped back and looked up at the darkening sky to find my center, but my stomach dropped.

With the blaring diamond lights and smack dab in the middle of Perrin, there wasn't a star in sight. The sky was pitch black and suddenly, I felt even more alone than I had before.

Lorraine was nowhere to be found.

The next swing I took cracked my resolve as the ball connected with the bat and soared out to left field above the heads of all their outfielders. I was numb to the excitement happening behind me in the dugout, everyone hollering for me to run. So I did, but not in the direction I should have.

Leaving first base behind, I jogged to the edge of the field and hopped the fence toward the bleachers, where Mary sat with her brother and a few of his friends.

"What the hell are you doing, Cody?" Tyson snapped with his arm pointed toward the chorus of angry chanting happening from my teammates and coaches.

"Can I have your keys?" I asked her with my hand out.

Mary's head cocked to the side.

"Get back in the fucking game, Cody!" Tyson growled and tried to break the attention I was giving his sister.

"*Please*," my voice cracked as the word came out, and she gently set the key chain in my palm. "Thank you," I said with a nod and took off toward the parking lot.

"What the hell are you doing?" My father's voice rang out as I passed him and my brother. They jumped down from the bleachers and followed me, but I ignored his order to stop as my eyes scanned the lot for Mary's dark red Toyota.

"Ryan!" His voice barked through the sound of upset.

"I can't see her! The stars, they're covered!" I yelled back.

"What the… are you high?" My dad snapped.

"No!" I yelled back, my eyes still scanning the cars up and down as my heart raced out of my chest. "The lights, the sound, the game… none of it matters!"

"It's your future, Ryan! That's all that matters."

"No, because it drowns her out. The lights are too bright, the noise is too loud…" I whirled on him. "The game doesn't matter if she's not here and she isn't."

"You're talking about the Mayor's girl again, aren't you?" He sighed and pulled off his cowboy hat, resting it on his hip with a grim expression.

"You can beat my ass about it later, Dad. I have somewhere to be, and it's not here," I growled at him.

"Ryan, stop," he snapped. "You're never gonna be good enough for that family. You're a poor farmer's kid, and you just ruined the only shot you had at making a life for yourself. You're acting like a goddamn fool!" He stepped forward, and I widened my stance, ready for the blow as I put my hands out to stop him.

"If you ever loved me, even for a split second the day I was born, then you'll let me do this. Because it may not seem like the right decision for *you*, but it's the only decision for *me*." I explained to him, but his angry expression held tight in his brows and jaw, never softened.

"Get back on the field, Ryan." He said with a tight snarl.

"No," I said, checking the sky once more for the stars.

Twinkling brighter than ever above my head was the North Star.

I lowered my gaze, the red paint of Mary's car coming into view, "I have to get home."

He lunged for me, but I was too fast. My cleats on the pavement were loud as I raced toward the car. The weight of my future on my tail but the suffocating pressure of my dreams weighed on my chest. I could hear the team yelling as I popped the door of her car open and climbed inside, the silence jarring as I closed the door.

I turned the engine over and peeled from the parking lot.

I waited with my breath held for the truck's headlights behind me as I sped onto the single-lane highway home, but they never came. He didn't follow me. I slowed down to a reasonable speed and loosened my grip on the wheel, but my heart was still pounding out of my chest. Out here, without the pesky lights from the city, I could see the sky painted with stars. I could feel her again.

"I'm coming," I whispered.

It took me less than three hours to get home. I had small bouts of speeding, and nothing about the way I drove was safe, but as I pulled up to her gated community, I knew it had all been for a reason. The game was blaring over the radio, and the boys had managed to win the game without me, just like Coach said.

They had never needed me.

But Lorraine did.

I could feel it in my bones, in the tightly charged muscles that corded together under my too-hot skin. Every nerve was buzzing, and my heart pounded.

Her house was dark, and for a moment, I thought I was wrong, that maybe they weren't home. But as I shut off the engine and the moon's light spread across her yard, I saw her.

Her face was pressed to the telescope just like that night, her messy short hair stuffed under a beanie to keep her ears warm in the breeze. Her face was more hollow than before, and I couldn't tell if it was the moon playing tricks or the pale color of her skin, but she looked sick. The desperate feeling to fix everything seeped into every crack within my body as I climbed from the car and started the slow walk up her driveway.

"What are you doing?" The wind threatening to steal the sound of my voice as I asked her the same question I had the first day I saw her. Her body stiffened, and she looked up at me.

FIELD

"Go away," I said. But there was no malice or fight to my words. Not that time.

I hadn't expected to see him. My shaky fingers found the knob of the radio and silenced it before the game even started because I was so heartbroken that I couldn't be there.

But now he was standing on my driveway in his pinstripe baseball uniform, dirty strands of hair sticking out the bottom of his backward-turned hat and that stupid nervous grin on his face. My brows furrowed as I did the math.

It was nearly three hours from Perrin.

There was no way he had played in that game and stood here with me.

It wasn't possible.

"No." He shook his head and reached up to pull off his hat, tucking it into his back pocket.

"You shouldn't be here if my dad—" I started but the soft shake of his head told me that excuse wasn't going to work.

It had been a very rough few days. I'd collapsed on Monday, unable to carry the weight of my own body, and it wasn't a second thought for us to end up at the hospital doing tests. The inner corners of my arms were still sore from all the needles they had shoved under my skin, and my muscles were still stiff from the confinements of a hard hospital mattress.

Food had become more unappetizing again, and the siren call of my bed was echoing in my head every time I made a move to work out the cramps forming. I'd taken a long shower, the steam forcing me to sit on the edge of the bath until the dizziness passed.

But when Ryan showed up on the driveway it returned tenfold, rushing through my tired body like an unstoppable tidal wave. The sight of him was enough to make me cry.

"I don't give a shit about your Dad, Starlight," Ryan chuckled and stepped forward until he was at the foot of the stairs, his balance uneasy and his shoulders pinned back with nerves. "Are you alright?" He asked me casually as if he could solve whatever issue left my lips next.

"No," I answered honestly, even though it's probably not what he wants to hear at the moment.

"When did you get home?" Ryan asked. It was clear that he wanted to come closer and desperately needed to close the gap between us, but he wouldn't do it unless I asked him to.

"This morning." I knotted my fingers around the hem of my sweater. It wasn't overly cold outside, even with the breeze. June's heat was starting to settle around the town, and all summer flowers had bloomed, making the air sticky and floral. But my body didn't care what temperature it was outside. My bones were frozen, and my circulation was shot.

"Is it bad?" He asked.

"It could be. I have an infection that's not healing on its own..." I trailed off. "You don't want to know all of this crap, Ryan."

He surged up the steps at my dismissal. "I want to know everything all the time," he argued, his hands flexing at his side from the incessant urge to touch me.

"They have me on medicine." My voice was tight and quiet to keep the dry, cracking sound from reaching him. "If it works, I'll be okay," I said, not looking away from him.

"*If*," Ryan repeated, his eyes glassy from holding back his emotions. "If it doesn't?" He asked.

"Then I go back in for more tests and treatment. The hospital is sterile. It's the best place for me, but I hate it there. It's so quiet except for this low hum that my brain knows is the machine but for some reason, I associate the sound to *death*." I swallowed hard and finally looked away from him.

"But being here, being home, might make you sick?" He questioned.

"Yeah," I nodded, "But that chance exists anywhere. It's just easier for my mother if I'm there, where she barely has to look after me." I sighed, trying to fill my lungs with air, but they were sore, and each breath was precious energy.

I could see the anger behind his eyes as he registered what I was saying to him. "You left the game..." I said next, my brows coming together in a tight line. "Everyone was there for *you*."

He was quiet for a moment that felt like forever, no doubt running the information over more than once. When he finally spoke again, I flinched at the sound. "I couldn't find you tonight," he said with a little shake.

Guilt ate at me, gnawing at my racing heart.

"I couldn't go to the game; there are too many people and a higher risk of worse infection," I explained, but his brows crinkled, and he shook his head no at me.

"No, no...I couldn't find you in the sky, and I know how ridiculous that sounds, but when I looked up, I couldn't find you." He reiterated with a heavy tone. "I hated it. You are literally the light I look for, and the past few days,... not knowing what was happening. I couldn't bear it, Rae. You gotta..." He stopped again, struggling to get it out.

Ryan's hands began to shake, and he could barely look at me anymore, tears welling in those striking green eyes without his permission as he chewed at his bottom lip. I reached out the moment he sank to his knees, his body heaving in upset with his palms flat against the porch. I crouched next to him, pulling him with what little strength I had until he was pressed against my chest, and we were nothing but a tight, tangled mess of each other.

His hat came loose in the contact and clattered to the ground as I raked my fingers into his hair and brushed them down against his wet cheek. His hands were tight against my back, fingers spread wide and pressed into my skin as if he was in threat of being blown away.

Ryan stiffened, his forehead resting against my shoulder. "You have to tell me everything. You can't just leave..." He said up a little and cupped my face in his calloused hands. "I want to help, and I know that I don't have any idea what you're up against, but I don't want you to go in it alone, so just..." he pressed our foreheads together. "You have to promise me that you won't do it alone."

I wasn't even sure that was a promise I could make; we were seventeen years old and I was a ticking time bomb. Part of my hesitation was rooted firmly in Ryan's reaction to a simple cold: if anything worse were to happen... How could I promise him that I wouldn't do it alone? I didn't want to share my suffering or pain with him. I wanted to protect him from that. To shield him from all of the bad in my life, he carried enough of his own around on his shoulders. And here he was on his knees, begging to take more.

"You have a future, Ryan," I whispered to him.

"Not without you, I don't," his answer was instant. "Stop trying to figure out how to push me away. I'm not leaving, Rae. Sick, healthy." He squeezed his hands tighter around my face. "You're mine, I'm yours."

"You can't ruin your dreams for some sick girl who might not see her eighteenth birthday, Ryan. I won't let you." I covered his hands with my own and pressed down.

"You're so cold," he whispered, the pain on his face evident as he struggled to gain control of his racing heart and strung-out emotions. "And I'm not ruining my dreams. You're a part of them now. I'm going to be a star, just like you." He kissed my nose. "And we're going to get out of this town and celebrate every birthday like it's your last. I'm going to buy you a stupid trinket every year. We're going to have six kids." He said with a smile.

"Ryan!" A small, defeated laugh fell from me, and he pouted at my protest. "Let's start with one," I chewed my bottom lip and scrunched my nose up at him. I couldn't help but give into his whims, his *love*.

"With your eyes and smile," he nipped at my nose with his teeth before kissing my cheek and then the corner of my mouth and jaw. "Promise?"

"Promise."

EPILOGUE

2022

The path down the lookout had grown over, and the weeds tangled together with the roots under the soles of my boots. Kids didn't appreciate make-out spots like they used to. I sighed, tugging out my cell phone, and used the flash to light my way.

"There you are," I muttered to no one but the cool air and restless wildlife. I inhaled slowly, my lungs never really filling with air. I was drowning on dry land. I was not sure I was ready for the walk ahead of me, but I knew I had to take it for the both of us. Each step up the steep path felt like my heart was shattering again.

We had known a day like today would come.

We always had.

The selfish idiot in me wanted more time.

It felt like there had never been enough hours in the day to love her.

But I couldn't control the time passing, and the things I could control I let slip through my fingers in a grief-filled blindness that threatened to ruin everything she worked so hard to give me. I stopped just before the opening, pressing my hand to a tree to steady myself, my eyes already welling with tears, my chest heaving with exhaustion, my throat dry and sticky with guilt. I bit down on my tongue just to feel something other than the swallowing sensation of overwhelming loneliness. I closed my eyes, hearing her laugh in the back of my mind, remembering how nervous she had been the first time I had shown her my spot. How tiny her body felt against mine as she tensed up and wouldn't take another step. *Just a little further.*

The path broke open to that vast clearing perched above the town in complete darkness and welcoming silence.

And finally, I could breathe.

The air stung as it went down, nipping at my lungs and reminding me I was alive.

"Hey, Starlight," I whispered, looking at the night stars and watching them burst across the sky like she was greeting me back. "It's weird being up here without you chewing my ear off about the stars, but you became one of them, just like I always knew you would."

The funeral had been brutal. People that I barely knew showed up, and the ones that should have been there, I couldn't find the courage to call. I wanted to give them all another week, another month without the immense grief of losing her. It was selfish, and I knew that, but I couldn't stop myself from *protecting people*, even if I were doing it the wrong way. Mary was going to be pissed when she found out, and I wasn't entirely in the mood to take an earful from her, no matter how right she'll be.

Cael wasn't speaking to me again. I had gotten in the car at the cabin and drove all the way to Texas, sleeping in a few shitty motels before rolling into town in three-day-old clothes and puffy eyes.

I walked to the cliff's edge and sat down in the spot I had been sitting in for twenty-some years. Only it felt cold without her shoulder brushing against mine. "I came up here to tell you how much I love you, but I think you already know that better than anyone. I saw Mary on the way into town. She didn't see me, but she was selling flowers from the back of her truck."

I pressed my tongue to the side of my lip and inhaled a shaky breath. "She still sells those massive lavender bundles. She had a little cardboard sign that told people she was sold out. I don't know how long I sat there just watching her smile and laugh with people. And I don't even have the courage to tell her that you're gone. She's going to be devastated, Rae. How dare you make me tell her," I gritted my teeth together.

"Saw Robert too. He's still on the farm. His wife gave birth to twins. I promised to talk to him more. He said Riona and Rory visited lots.... It made me feel guilty, but something about that place made me feel suffocated. They named one of the twins Rain. He said it wasn't for you, but I could see it in his eyes how much he missed you, too. We all do. You were too good to all of us Cody kids. We didn't deserve that kindness half the time."

I remember the days she spent on the farm when I couldn't get away, playing with my siblings in the long grass while Robert and I did chores. I missed the way her laughter floated through the grass, and the way her skin was freckled-kissed after a day in the sun.

Giving her useless updates on life, my family, and our family seemed useless most of the time, but just talking lifted an invisible weight off my chest. It was hard to do that with anyone anymore; my office walls got the blunt of my frustrated one-shots and disgruntled sighs.

"Riona is doing a good job taking care of Cael." my brows knitted together. I was mad at myself for letting his life become what it had. Chaos, drugs, parties... Riona had explained it that he was seeking a high that couldn't come from oral ingestion but rather something that his mind couldn't produce for him after the death of Lorraine.

Happiness.

She told me that it wasn't something we could just give him, that handing over half-assed niceties and fake interest would only make the distance grow. Cael was too smart for my bullshit. A fake smile and a dad joke weren't going to cut it.

He had grown up with Lorraine as a mother. There was no competition.

"I remember the day that funny-looking boy was born like it was yesterday. What a lanky baby," I laughed. "With his giant blue eyes and full head of blonde hair. He's always been the best of both of us."

I paused, trying to contain the wave of emotion that rolled through me. "His heart never stopped growing, Rae. It's too big for this world, and it gets him in so much trouble because he just doesn't know when to stop."

Sounds like someone else I know.

I could hear her scolding me for the remark, knowing full well that she'd scolded me for it countless times. *Give him a break. He's just like his daddy. When he sets his mind on something, he won't stop until he has it.*

"I don't know how to protect him from the world without making him hate me. Seems like everything I do is wrong, but I just—" I stopped, running my hands through my hair with a heavy sigh. "I'm losing him, Rae. He's slipping through my fingers, and I don't know what to do."

It wasn't the first time I had spoken those words. It certainly wouldn't be the last. Raising a son like Cael was like climbing a slippery mountain without a rope. You could only hope that the next thing your hand grasped onto was a ledge wide enough to perch on as you caught your breath.

I had screwed up before. I would screw up again. I knew that, and as if Lorraine was cementing the statement, the wind kicked up through the trees, and I sighed. Maybe raising Cael wasn't about how I could do it, or Riona, or himself. But caring for him the way she had, the way she had for all of us.

It had never been easy for us, coming out the gate with our relationship and the ups and downs of her illness. We had never walked a well-paved road. Her father hated me until the day he died, her mother even more. But Lorraine held true. She never cared what they thought. She went to school. She got a degree and worked in the school right there in town until the day we left. My dad died shortly after I graduated, never even saw me play my first game in the minors. Everyone else came, Lorraine rounded up anyone she could.

It felt good to step back on the field, and for a while, my career was promising. We got married in a small church with only a handful of people around, and not long after, Mary dragged Landry down the aisle. We bought houses across from each other, and our little family was exactly what we had all been craving for our entire lives. It finally felt like we didn't have to flee that shitty town like we had made it somewhere we wanted to be.

When March rolled around, I was knee-deep in baseball, and suddenly, Lorraine and Mary were sicker than dogs. It took Landry longer to connect the dots, but it seemed both our wives were pregnant.

It felt like a whirlwind, "the world hasn't stopped moving since, Rae." I mumbled to myself and the stars. "They were born together, and no matter how hard I tried..."

They belong together. A collision of stars. It's romantic, Ryan.

I could hear her whispering.

"Eta Carinae." I nodded with a smile. "I hate that even in death, you're always right."

The wind pushed through the surrounding trees again, and it caused a funny laugh to bubble up from my sore chest. "I thought separating them would help them thrive. Being together, they could only reach so far. But I might have been wrong, Starlight. I might have snuffed out whatever of your light was left in Cael."

I'm too stubborn to admit I was wrong and too sad to pretend like I have the energy to fight with him. "I'm stuck between standing in his path or letting him run himself into the ground, and I don't know what will be worse. He never wants to talk to me, and I don't blame the kid. I wasn't there for him when I should have been.

"I know we made a promise, Rae, I know..." I choked up on the words. "I know you didn't want me there..."

I could hear her words in my head, clear as day.

"Promise me Ryan. Promise you won't come see me. I can't–" she stopped, choking on the pain that flooded her chest. *"I don't want you to remember me like that. You have to promise me to stay away."*

"I'm not making a promise as stupid as that Rae," I shook my head and grabbed her face in my hands brushing the tears that fell to her cheeks with the pads of my thumbs. *"I'm not letting you die alone."*

"I won't be alone, I'll have the boys there. But you can't come, you can't remember me like that. Sick and dying... I won't let you." She said with conviction, the strength waning in her voice.

"It's not up to you." I argued, so sick of her need to protect me. I was begging her to protect herself, just this once.

"If you don't promise me, I'll call Mary, she'll take me home. I'll force your goodbye, don't do that to us. You can't let your love die with me." She said.

SO LONG, HONEY

*"You're doing this to us, how am I supposed to look that boy in the eye and tell him that his Mama **asked** for this? Begged for it!"* I snapped, losing my temper and immediately regretting it when I saw the look on her tired face. *"I'm sorry. I'm just scared, Starlight. This is scary."*

"I know, baby. But I can't ask that of our boy, our baby. I can't keep him away." She hummed, *"I need you to say goodbye now, when we can do it and I can remember it. When **you** can remember it. Don't do it when I can't hear you. Please, Ry."*

"I don't want to say goodbye," I growled, sinking to my knees at her side. *"I can't...I can't do this without you. Raise Cael, raise myself..."* I don't even know when the tears started, *"You're all I've known."*

"You've loved me so loudly for so long that you don't know how to love anyone else but Cael is ours and he needs you. Like I needed you to fill all the broken spaces with your love, you've done such a good job but I won't let you watch the light die in me, not when Cael burns bright. He's your star now, baby. Follow the sun back into the light."

"Cael burns bright," I hummed, remembering her words. Even now in the middle of so much grief, like a supernova that boy burned.

"You know, he doesn't sleep anymore, and when he's not crying he's yelling at me for abandoning you. I just...Maybe I spent too much time sneaking around to avoid his questions, Rae. I couldn't look him in the eye without seeing you and all that heartbreak." I bit down hard on my lip to steady my breathing.

"It was painful, living through that twice over. I couldn't do it anymore. I'm sorry I wasn't here when you left. I wish I had been there. I shouldn't have listened to you, I should have just come. It was cruel for you to ask that of me." I stared up at the sky for a long moment and inhaled.

Now I was arguing with the stars.

I rubbed my hands over my face and exhaled a heavy breath.

"I'll do better by the boy Rae, at least I'll try. I'll never be able to fill your shoes, but..."

The stars seemed to surge brighter back at me for a split second.

"I'll try." I pressed my fingers to my chest, tapping with what little energy I had left to show her that I would be okay, closed my eyes, and cried.

Acknowledgements

There is not a day that goes by that I don't cry over something stupid, I'm a weepy bitch and I've cried for an entire putting Honey Pot and So Long Honey together. 365 days of immense grief flowing into these books and they're so heavy, and I'm so sorry. Everyone always asks me what character I relate to the most and everyone always expects my answer to be Arlo, because he's a black cat but it's not him. And even though I've never battled with addiction, or crashed a car, and my coping mechanism for my grief are a little healthier. I've always been Cael. I love too loud, too fast and burn out even faster. My emotions rule my common sense but I'm a damn good listener and I will do anything to make sure the people around me are never sad, even if it means I have to be sad in silence.

I lost my Lorraine, that person who matched my loud every single god damn day. Even when I wanted to be sad in silence she was in my inbox yapping about something stupid or demanding photos of her great grand kids. To the point that I cry every time I create an album on facebook knowing that in 2.5 seconds there won't be a barrage of notifications on every single one of those photos. She shared her life with everyone so loudly and with such pride that sometimes you were like, dear god woman you shouldn't have said that. But she didn't care because even the worst of her stories were teaching moments. I miss strawberry shortcake on my birthdays and spending too much money on making Halloween DIYs that she sent me every morning. (and I mean 365 days of Halloween crafts). I miss watching hockey and not being sad when I do because I cry every time I pick up my phone to send her a message she'll never see about Sidney Crosby. I miss that every time we hung up the phone, she'd tell me she loved me but she'd always say; *"Stay gold Shickster"* because of my obsession with the Outsiders in grade 9 that I made my whole personality for my entire life.

I just really miss her, and these books were a way to heal from that.

So my thank you this time is to the readers. Thank you for giving me grace and time to overcome the mountain of grief that my Bubbe left behind for me to climb. I can't thank you enough for loving these horribly sad and broken characters even in their darkness moments and for still being there for them when they climb out of those shadows and become the people they are today. Thank you for loving me in the same circumstance. And if you're still here, and you're still sad, it's okay to be that way. Let yourself be sad, misery loves misery and I'll be here when you're read. Here's to character growth and healing our broken hearts with glitter glue and self-deprecating internet memes.

Love Shic (Aubrey)

www.ingramcontent.com/pod-product-compliance
Lightning Source LLC
Chambersburg PA
CBHW060614080526
44585CB00013B/820